MW00709572

PETS' NAMES
OF THE RICH AND FAMOUS

By Robert Davenport

Publisher: W. Quay Hays
Managing Editor: Colby Allerton
Design: Catherine Vo Bailey
Copy Editor: Peter Hoffman

All views and opinions contained herein are solely those of the authors.

For information:
General Publishing Group, Inc.
2701 Ocean Park Boulevard, Suite 140,
Santa Monica, California, 90405

Notice: The information in this book is true and complete to the best of our
knowledge. It is offered with no guarantees on the part of the authors or
General Publishing Group, Inc. Authors and publisher disclaim all liability in
connection with the use of this book.

ISBN 1-881-649-27-X: $5.95

Library of Congress Catalog
Card Number 95-75053

Published by General Publishing Group, Inc.,
Los Angeles, CA

10 9 8 7 6 5 4 3 2 1

Bound and printed in the United States of America

TABLE OF
CONTENTS

PREFACE

What is the first thing that you do when you buy a pet? Name it! And that's why everyone with a new pet needs a pet name book. It's much harder to name a pet than a baby, since most people don't name their cat after their grandfather or maiden aunt.

While some pet name books give you lists of what the author thinks might be a good name for a pet, this is the only pet name book exclusively dedicated to those names which people have actually bestowed upon a pet. And what a list! These aren't just any old people. These pet owners are the most famous in history, from Presidents of the United States to heroes to motion picture and television stars, each pet owner in this book has a name which is instantly recognizable. This is the most comprehensive list of celebrity pets ever assembled. If you don't find your favorite celebrity listed in the book, it doesn't mean that we've missed them. A lot of famous people, for reasons known only to themselves, do not have any pets.

The names in this book were in most cases supplied by the celebrity themselves, or children who were there at the same time that the pets were. You will find insights into the pet naming practices of celebrities, including those who name their pets after their famous roles (guess who owns Kirk and Conan) or hits (see Sadie and Heartlight No. 1). There are also humorous choices, like the singer who named his cat Bing Clawsby or the actress who named her cats Joan Pawford and Kitty Dearest.

This is the first edition, but it won't be the last. If you know the name of the pet of a famous person, send it along to the following address. We'll make sure it's included in the next edition. Send the name of the pet, along with the celebrity owner, to:

Robert Davenport
Pets' Names of the Rich and Famous
Post Office Box 1989
Beverly Hills, CA 90213-1989

ACKNOWLEDGMENTS

I would like to thank Quay Hays, Colby Allerton, and Harlan Boll of the General Publishing Group for their faith in this project, and my agent Jim Pinkston for bringing it to their attention.

In addition, I would like to thank the following persons and organizations who assisted in the research of the book:

Kareem Abdul-Jabbar, Actors and Others For Animals, Edie Adams, Kirstie Alley, Amanda Foundation, Harry Anderson, Lucie Arnaz, Mary Kay Ash, Ed Asner, Rene Auberjonois, Gene Autry, Catherine Bach, Orson Bean, Amanda Bearse, Jim Belushi, Candice Bergen, Valerie Bertinelli, Pat Boone, Ray Bradbury, Barbara Taylor Bradford, Mel Brooks, Ken Burns, Danton Burroughs (Edgar Rice Burroughs), Dean Cain, K Callan, David Cassidy, William Christopher, Dick Clark, Glenn Close, Shane Conrad, Bill Cosby, Chris Costello (Lou Costello), Wes Craven, Christina Crawford, Tom Cruise, Bette Davis, Doris Day, Bo Derek, Susan Dey, Walt Disney Archives, Robert Duvall, Clint Eastwood, Elvira, Nanette Fabray, Jeffray Fargher, Mrs. Debbie Fields, Carrie Fisher, John Forsythe, Michael J. Fox, Mary Frann, Jennie Garth, Estelle Getty, Leeza Gibbons, Theresa Goldston, Phil Gonzalez, Billy Graham, Melanie Griffith, Larry Hankin, Valerie Harper, Mary Hart, Mariette Hartley, David Hasselhoff, Tippi Hedren, Charlton Heston, Dustin Hoffman, Earl Holliman, Hollywood Park, Bob Hope, Whitney Houston, Marty Ingels, Michael Jackson, Malcolm-Jamal Warner, Shirley Jones, Alex Karras, Michael Keaton, Howard Koch, Harvey Korman, Alan Ladd, Jr., Steve Lawrence, Stan Lee, Jay Leno, Bela Lugosi, Jr., Roddy McDowall, Matthew Margolis, Cheech Marin, Garry Marshall, Steve Martin, Burgess Meredith, Mary Ann Mobley, Demi Moore, Mary Tyler Moore, Jack Nicholson, PAWS LA, Dolly Parton, Gregory Peck, People for the Ethical Treatment of Animals (PETA), Vincent Price, Purina, Julia Roberts, Ginger Rogers, Wayne Rogers, Santa Anita, Bob Selleck (Tom Selleck), William Shatner, Sally Struthers, John Tesh, Tiffani-Amber Thiessen, Courtney Thorne-Smith, Roger Valentine, Reginald VelJohnson, Steve Wayland, David L. Wolper, Michael York.

ABOUT THE AUTHOR

Robert Davenport has written *The Rich and Famous Baby Name Book, Pets' Names of the Rich and Famous,* and *The Celebrity Almanac.* Robert has also been the editor of the last three editions of the *Hereditary Society Blue Book.*

Mr. Davenport is a graduate of Middlebury College (B.A.), St. John's Law School (J.D.), Harvard Business School (M.B.A.), and USC Film School. During Vietnam, he was a Naval Flight Officer, commanding a combat aircrew with Patrol Squadron Forty-Four, and during the Persian Gulf War he was an officer in the U.S. Army JAG Corps. After law school, he worked for the U.S. Department of Justice in Washington, D.C., and after business school he worked at various entertainment companies, including CBS, Viacom, New World Pictures, and Twentieth Century-Fox. He currently makes his home in Los Angeles with his cat Rocky.

DOG

NAMES

ABAKARU	Cheops
ABEL	Cheryl Ladd
ABNER	Cokie Roberts
ACERO	Earle Jorgensen
AELLO	Actaeon
AGAMEMNON	Maurice Sendak
AGATHA	Lesley Gore
AGNES	Louise Shaffer
AGRE	Actaeon
AIWA	Bo Derek
AJAX	King Edward VIII
ALADDIN	Pinocchio
ALBERT	Jaclyn Smith
ALCE	Actaeon
ALICE	Linda Blair
	Dick Clark
ALL SPICE	Della Reese
	Fred Astaire
ALOMA	Gladys, Duchess of Marlborough
AMANDA	George Cukor
AMBER	Ray Aghayan
	Bo Derek
	Jenilee Harrison
	Bob Mackie

Celebrity designer Bob Mackie admits that his Lhasa Apso's are typical Beverly Hills pooches, "They go to the hairdresser more than most women I know."

AMBRIGET	Jonathan Prince
AMOS	Andy Warhol
AMY	H. R. Haldeman
ANDY	Charles Schultz
ANGEL	Digby Diehl
	Jerry Lewis
	Aaron Spelling
ANGIE	Esther Williams
ANNABELLE	Stan Lee
ANNIE	Barbara Eden
	John Glover
APOLLO	Sherman Hemsley
	Robbin Masters
APOLLON	King Arthur
APRIL	Jenilee Harrison
ARCHIE	Terry Thomas
	Valerie Harper
	Ed Koch
	Andy Warhol
ARGOS	Odysseus

When Odysseus returned in disguise after being gone for twenty years in the Trojan War, his faithful dog Argos wagged his tail, the only one in the house to recognize him. Odysseus, not yet ready to reveal his identity, had to ignore him, and Argos died of grief on the spot.

ARGUS	Actaeon
	Albert Payson Terhune
	Gene Tierney

ARIZONA   Oprah Winfrey

ARLO   Erma Bombeck

ARNO   Errol Flynn

Errol Flynn's dog Arno met a watery end when he fell overboard from Flynn's yacht and drowned. When gossip columnist Jimmy Fidler made fun of Errol in his column for not saving his pooch, Flynn tracked Fidler down at his favorite watering hole and beat him up.

ARROW   Patty Hearst

ARTHUR PENDRAGON
    Charlton Heston

ASBOLUS   Actaeon

ASHLEY   Chick Hearn
    Richard Simmons

Richard Simmons doesn't like to neuter his pets. He thinks this makes them go through an attitude change and that they become much meaner. Good thinking, Richard!

ASTA   Nick Charles

There really was an Asta, before the *Thin Man* books and movies. The real Asta belonged to Laura Perelman, with whom author Dashiell Hammet was having an affair. This affair did not please either Mr. Perelman, Laura's

husband, nor Lillian Hellman, who was Hammet's lover.

ASTOR   Burt Reynolds

ASTRO   Elroy Jetson
    Monica Seles

ASTRONAUT   Luci Johnson

ATMO   Princess Stephanie

ATTICUS
    Sen. George McGovern

George McGovern nominated Tom Eagleton as his VP when he was running for President in 1972, then had to withdraw the nomination. Signs immediately were everywhere reading "Atticus for Vice President." However, after the Eagleton affair, Atticus decided it was better to be a pet than a politician, and declined to run.

AUSTIN   Tommy Lasorda

AUTIE MURPHY   Doris Day

AUTUMN   Doris Day

BABIL   Queen Alexandra

BABY   Eva Gabor

BABY BOY   Liberace

Liberace was completely devoted to Baby Boy, whom he thought of as a person and not an animal. Each night, his French Poodle would join him for dinner, sitting at the dining room table in his own chair, eating his dinner with Liberace off his own sterling silver bowl engraved with his name, and wearing his own special jeweled collar.

BABY DAUPHINE
                    Karen Kelly

BABY DOLL
                    Tennessee Williams

BABY JANE   Richard Florio
                    Daniel Kapavik

BABY LION   Eva Gabor

BABYLAS   Gladys, Duchess
                    of Marlborough

BACCHUS   Gladys, Duchess
                    of Marlborough

BAGEL   Barry Manilow

BAGHERA   Colette

BAGLE   Tracy Bregman

BALTO   Gunnar Kasson

Visitors to New York might wonder why there is a bronze statute of Balto in Central Park. It was put there to honor his heroic trek leading Gunnar Kasson's dog team through a horrible blizzard to deliver serum to Nome, Alaska during the diphtheria epidemic of 1925.

BAMBI   Gene Kelly

BAMBINA   Franco Zeffirelli

BANCO   Francoise Sagan

BANDIT   Carrie Snodgress
                    Betty White

BANDY   Betty White

BANG   David Lloyd George

BANQUO   Anais Nin

BARCLAY   Amanda Bearse

BARK   Bill Murray

BARNABY   Bill Blass

BARNEY   Thom Bray
                    Christian Slater

BARNEY MILLER   Doris Day

BARON   Louis J. Camuti
                    Richard Todd

BARRON   Jimmy Stewart

Jimmy Stewart has never been without a dog. Once, when on the Johnny Carson show, he brought Johnny and the audience to tears with a very sentimental poem he had written about one of his dogs.

BARRY   Bert Lahr

BASHER   Lorenzo Lamas

BASKET   Gertrude Stein
                    Alice B. Toklas

BEAGLE   Lyndon Johnson

BEAN   Jimmy Barker

BEANS   Robert Vaughn

BEAR   Stefanie Powers

Stefanie Powers is an animal rights activist, and carries on the work in Africa of the

William Holden Foundation.

Reginald VelJohnson

BEARFACE   Bijan

BEATY   King Edward VII

BEAU

General Omar Bradley
William Cowper

William Cowper featured his own spaniel Beau in *The Dog and the Water Lily* and *On a Spaniel Called Beau Killing a Young Bird*.

Dina Schmidt
Anson Williams

Anson Williams named his production company Basset Productions after his dogs.

BEAU BRUMMELL

Armand Deutsch

BEAU JANGLES

Carol Burnett

BEAUTY   Corey Feldman
David Lloyd George

The black chow of David Lloyd George, Beauty was famous for her dancing skills at the parties of the English Prime Minister.

Arthur Taxier

BEBE   Reginald VelJohnson

BELA   Elvira

BELLA   John Larroquette

BELLE   Arthur Treacher

BELLE AUDE   Colette

BELSHAZZAR   Billy Graham

Billy Graham named his dog Belshazzar after a king in the Bible, who gave a great feast for a thousand lords. Every time the Grahams saw Belshazzar eat they felt as though they were feeding a thousand lords.

BELVA   Theda Bara

BEN   Steffi Graf

BEPPO   Queen Victoria
E. B. White

BERNARDO   Dick Clark

BERT   Michael Landon

BERTHA LOU   Bruce James

BERTHE   Cole Porter

BESSIE   Calvin Coolidge
Jennifer Jason Leigh

BETTY   Penny Marshall

BETTYSAN   Gladys, Duchess
of Marlborough

BEVERLY

Betsy Bloomingdale

BIANCA   Jennifer Capriati
Paul King
Elaine Princi

BIG BEN   Herbert Hoover

BIGGEST   Doris Day

BIJOU   Queen Alexandra

BILL   Frances Day

Cloris Leachman

BILLY THE KID
Valerie Harper

BINGLEY   Tomie De Paola

BINGO   Agatha Christie

BINKY   Betty White

BIRD   Robin Wright

BISCUIT   Barry Manilow
Patrick Wayne

BISMARK   Shannen Doherty
David Lloyd George

BLACK TOOTH   Soupy Sales

BLACK WATCH MOON-
STRUCK   Bill Cosby

BLACKBERRY
Calvin Coolidge

BLACKIE   Eva Gabor
Ernest Hemingway
John F. Kennedy
Elke Sommer
John Wayne

BLANCH   King Lear

BLANCO   Lyndon Johnson

BLAZE
Franklin Delano Roosevelt

FDR created quite a public scandal when his bull mastiff bumped a serviceman from a military flight home, but it was only when Blaze bit Fala that FDR had him destroyed.

BLEMIE   Eugene O'Neill

BLEU   King Louis IX

BLIX   A. J. Cronin

BLONDI   Adolf Hitler

BLONDIE   Earl Holliman

BLUCHER
George Armstrong Custer

General Custer's pets were also Indian fighters, and his staghound Blucher was killed by an arrow at the Battle of Washita.

BLUE   Katharine Ross

BLUE BANDIT   Eddie Velez

BNEITA   Gladys, Duchess
of Marlborough

BO
Eleanor "Cissy" Patterson
Jimmy Stewart

BOATSWAIN   Lord Byron

BOB   King George V
David Letterman
Randolph Scott

BOB DYLAN
Courtney Love

BOBBY   Clark Gable
Harold Lloyd

Harold Lloyd at one time had 65 Great Danes, whose baying became so loud at night that his neighbors in Beverly Hills forced him to build a kennel in Westwood to house them.

Albert Payson Terhune

BOBBY SOCKS
　　　　　　　Tracy Bregman

BOBO　　　　　　Doris Day
　　　　　　　　Bruce Lee

BOBOL　　　Franco Zeffirelli

BODIE　　Dr. James Herriot

BODRI　　　　　Bela Lugosi

BOGIE　　　　Dirk Bogarde
　　　　　　　Earl Holliman
　　　　　　　　Bo Hopkins

BOJANGLES
　　　　　　Sammy Davis, Jr.

BOLERO　　　　Bo Derek

BONES
　　Gen.George C. Marshall

BONNE　　　King Louis XIV

BONNIE　Tallulah Bankhead
　　　　　　　Diana Rigg
　　　　Tiffani-Amber Thiessen

BONSO　　　　Tom Brown

BOOJUM　　　Bette Davis

BOOMER　Barbara Mandrell

BOONE　　　Glen Campbell

BOOTIE　　　Betty White

BOOTS　　Charlie Chaplin
　　　　　　Joe Morrison
　　　　　　Jonathan Pryce

BOOTSIE　　　June Havoc
　　　　　　Gypsy Rose Lee

BORDEAUX　Anne Archer

BOROTRA
　　　　　Peggy Guggenheim

BOSCO　　Michael J. Fox

Michael J. Fox is closer to his dogs than to any woman. He said "It's something about dogs not talking back."

BOSTON BEANS
　　　　　Calvin Coolidge

BOUBOULE
　　　　Olivia De Havilland

BOUILLABAISSE
　　　　F. Scott Fitzgerald
　　　　　Zelda Fitzgerald

BOULDER　　Joan Van Ark

Joan Van Ark, who starred on TV's *Knots Landing*, shares something very personal with her Old English Sheepdog, Boulder. Each morning, they both have to have their hairdos blowdried, which they do together.

BOUNCE　　　King Arthur
　　　　　Alexander Pope

BOWS　　　Jimmy Barker

BOXCAR WILLIE
　　　　　Maureen Reagan

BOXEY　　　Anne Archer

BOY　　　　King Arthur
　　　　　Catfish Hunter
　　　　　Prince Rupert

BOZO　　　Roger A. Caras
　　　　　Jimmy Carter

BRAHM　　　　Elvira

BRAN　　　　King Arthur

BRANDY   Don Adams

BREAK
    Albert Payson Terhune

BRENTWOOD
      Brenda Vaccaro

BRIAR   Susan Dey

BRIN   Sir Wilfred Grenfel

BRINDLE   Brenda Vaccaro

BRISTOL   Dick Martin

BROTHER   Richard Pryor

BROWNIE   Jimmy Barker
    Mrs. Debbie Fields
    Vincent Price
    T. H. White

BRUCE
    Albert Payson Terhune

BRUISER   John D'Aquisto
    Burt Reynolds

BRUNO
    Kareem Abdul-Jabbar
    Greg Louganis

BRUT   Hugh O'Brian

BRUTUS   Bill Blass
    Charles Feldman

Hollywood super agent Charles Feldman, who numbered Marilyn Monroe among his clients, had his dog Brutus snatched in Capri. After being recovered in Naples, Brutus returned to a lavish welcome home party thrown by a well-to-do friend of Mr. Feldman.

    Charlton Heston
    Jean Howard
    Elvis Presley
    Lisa Marie Presley
    Reginald VelJohnson

BUBBLES   Doris Day
    Totie Fields

BUCEPHALUS
    Joanne Carson

BUCK   Janet Jackson
    Dorothy Jordan

BUCKY   Doris Day

BUDDY   John D'Aquisto
    Carrie Fisher
    Morris Frank
    John F. Kennedy
    Michael Landon

BUDDY MOZART
    Harvey Korman

BUDGY
   Franklin Delano Roosevelt

BUFFO   Tennessee Williams

BUFFY   Jason James Richter
    William Zabka

BULL   Sarah Bernhardt

BULLER   Beryl Markham

BULLET   Roy Rogers

Roy Rogers not only had Trigger, his wonder horse, but also a wonder dog Bullet. Both of them are immortalized at his museum, where they are stuffed and on display.

BULLWINKLE   Richard Paul

BULLY   Wallis Simpson
Queen Victoria

BUMPY   Beverly Sills

BUMPER   Halle Berry

BUNGA   Raymond Massey

Raymond Massey's Bunga at first brought home hedgehogs, rabbits and such, but it wasn't long before he was bringing home roast beef and turkey, fully cooked. Investigation revealed that a neighbor, who later abandoned the custom, was cooling food on her porch.

BUNGEY   King Arthur

BUNK   Dorothy Parker

BUNKER   A. J. Cronin

BUNTY   Pat O'Brien

BURNABY   Michael J. Fox

BUSTER   Kirstie Alley
Amanda Bearse
Sir Guy Standing

BUTCH   Michael Gray
Eleanor "Cissy" Patterson

BUTKUS   Sylvester Stallone

Sylvester Stallone wrote a part into the film *Rocky* for his bull mastiff Butkus, and he almost stole the show away from Sly.

BUTTERFLY   John F. Kennedy

BUTTON   Katharine Hepburn

BUTTONS   Jimmy Barker
Alex Haley
John Mitchell

BUZZY   Michael Gray

BYRON   Sean Astin
George Armstrong Custer

C. FRED BUSH George Bush

Millie got her idea to write a book from an earlier pet, when George Bush's dog C. Fred Bush published *A Dog's Life*.

C.D.   Emma Samms

CAACIE   Dwight D. Eisenhower

CAESAR   King Edward VII

King Edward VII's terrier Caesar had a simple inscription on his collar "I am Caesar, the king's dog." He became a national symbol as man's best friend when he followed his master's coffin in the funeral procession.

Beryl Markham
Orson Welles

CAJUN   Della Reese

CALABAN   Maureen McGovern

CALAMITY JANE
Calvin Coolidge

Will Rogers felt that the dogs were better fed than people at the White House. When Silent Cal invited him to dinner, he sat there starving, while great amounts of food were passed to the passel of dogs. Finally, in desperation, will got down on all fours and started barking.

CALIBAN   Julia Campbell

CALVIN
Harriet Beecher Stowe

CALYPSO   Liz Smith

CAMILLE   Helen Hayes
John James

CAMP   Sir Walter Scott

CANACHE   Actaeon

CANDIDA   Dirk Bogarde

CANDY   Bo Hopkins

CANUTE   Thomas Dewey
Vita Sackville-West

CAPTAIN   Harold Lloyd
Jeanette MacDonald
George Washington
Betty White

CAPTAIN BOBBY
Cloris Leachman

CARDIGAN
George Armstrong Custer

CARLO   Emily Dickinson

CARLOS   Bob Barker

Bob Barker runs Dog-A-Thons, in which stars parade their pets at a shopping mall in order to raise donations for the Morris Animal Foundation for research into animal diseases.

CARLOTTA   John Lehmann

John Lehmann's spaniel Carlotta was the toast of London, a feature at fashionable parties where she could regale guests with her varied repertoire of songs, although she was best known for her arias.

CARNOUSTIE   Joan Fontaine

CAROL   King George VI

CAROLINE   John Houseman

CARON   King Charles IX

CASEY   Eydie Gorme
Tim Holt
Steve Lawrence

For Steve Lawrence and his wife Eydie Gorme, their pets also celebrate Christmas. Their four dogs send out over 40 presents each year to fellow pets, including those of Bob Newhart, Perry Como and Frank Sinatra (whose parrot is always remembered). The gifts in past years have ranged from pillows to charms to dishes.

CASPER	Katie Wagner
CASSIE	Charles Bronson
	Jill Ireland
CASSY	David Cassidy
CASWELL LADDIE BOY	
	Warren G. Harding
	Woodrow Wilson
CATCHER	Kate Jackson
CAVALL	King Arthur
CENTIME	Natalie Wood
CESARE	Francesco Scavullo
CHABLIS	Kathie Lee Gifford
	Frank Gifford
CHAMP	Herb Alpert
	Tanya Roberts
	Edward G. Robinson
CHAMPION TINTERN TIP-	
TOE	Woodrow Wilson
CHANCE	Carol Lawrence
CHANG	Betty White
CHARCOAL	Bijan
CHARDONNAY	
	Kathie Lee Gifford
	Frank Gifford
CHARLEMAGNE	
	Jimmy Barker
CHARLES	Richard Thomas
CHARLEY	John Steinbeck

John Steinbeck's dog Charles le Chien, upon whom he based his book *Travels with Charley*, was a real French poodle, who actually responded best when addressed in his native French! It was only with great difficulty that he finally learned broken English.

CHARLIE	Bea Arthur
	Doris Day
	Sandy Duncan

Sandy Duncan's dog Charlie is such a city dog that when he is in the country he refuses to relieve himself on the grass, and insists on finding asphalt.

	Leeza Gibbons
	Caroline Kennedy
	Carol Lawrence
	Robert Wagner
CHARLIE BROWN	
	Red Buttons
	Nanette Fabray
	Earl Holliman
CHARLIE POTATOES	
	Robert Blake
CHARO	Helen Hayes
CHECKERS	Richard Nixon
CHELSEA	Dudley Moore
	Robert Wagner
CHEO	James Mason
CHESTER	Sally Struthers
CHEYENNE	Kelly McGillis
CHICO	Lou Costello
	John Lehmann

CHIEF
Albert Payson Terhune

CHILI Bobby Short

CHINA Joanne Carson
Bo Derek

CHING King George VI
Valerie Perrine

CHING CHING
Shirley Temple

CHING CHING II
Shirley Temple

CHINKAPEN
Lyndon Johnson

CHIPPER Doris Day

CHIQUITA Helen Hayes

CHLOE Judith Ivey

CHONG
David Lloyd George

The black chow of Prime Minister David Lloyd George was a regular participant in cabinet meetings, and her favorite at these was Winston Churchill.

CHOO-CHOO
King George VI

King George VI called his Tibetan Lion dog Choo-Choo because his barking sounded like a train.

CHOP SUEY Liberace

CHOPPER Ice-T

CHOU CHOU Judy Garland

CHOW MEIN Liberace

CHRIS John Galsworthy

CHRISSIE Shirley Jones

Shirley Jones doesn't just talk about helping animals, she is a regular volunteer with the Veterinary Society of America.

CHRISTABEL James Thurber

CHRISTY Henry Kravis
Connie Sellecca

Connie Sellecca and her husband John Tesh gave their son Gib a dog for Christmas, and that's why they all named him Christy.

Brooke Shields
John Tesh

CHRISTY LOVE
Holly Robinson

CHRYSTAL Billy Wilder

CHUCKIE Sally Struthers

CHULEH Beatrix Potter

CIF Bo Derek

CIGAR
Edward G. Robinson

CINDERELLA Ann Miller

CINDY Sid Caesar
Dian Fossey
J. Edgar Hoover
Garry Marshall

Garry Marshall, the creator of the TV series *Laverne and*

Shirley, was given a pooch by series star Cindy Williams which he named after her, and he featured the dog in the opening credits of the show.

| | Marilyn Monroe |
| CINEMA | John Buechler |

CINNAMON

	Truman Capote
	Joanne Carson
	Della Reese

CLANCY MULDOON
Shannen Doherty

CLEMENTINE
John Barrymore

CLEO	Gracie Allen
	Brooks Atkinson
	George Burns
	Edward J. DeBartolo, Jr.
	Charlton Heston
	Carol Lawrence

When Carol Lawrence was playing Maria on Broadway in *West Side Story*, she would always bring Cleo with her to the Winter Garden Theatre. Cleo knew she wasn't supposed to make a noise at the theatre, but the minute she got home she'd go crazy getting the barking out of her system.

| CLIPPER | John F. Kennedy |
| CLIQUOT | Joan Crawford |

Joan Crawford, in an obvious attempt to save money on monograms, gave her poodle the same initials as all of her adopted offspring, C.C., so that pooch Cliquot Crawford joined the ranks of children Christina, Christopher, Cathy, and Cynthia.

CLOVER
George Washington

CLOVIS LEE   David Bates

Even though artist David Bates' springer spaniel Clovis Lee doesn't have a tail, that doesn't stop David from doing oil paintings, brass sculptures and wood carvings of Clovis Lee with a tail. However, David's artistic endeavors are in spite of, rather than in cooperation with, Clovis Lee. One of the dog's favorite tricks is chewing on the paint tubes, and watching the paint spurt out.

CLOWN   Brigitte Bardot

Brigitte Bardot is an animal rights activist, and one of her crusades was the abolition of cruelty in slaughterhouses. As a result of her television appeals, the French passed a law they named the "BB Law" in her honor, which required them to use the more humane stun gun to kill the animals.

Don Rickles
Roger Vadim

CLUMSY King Arthur

CLYDE Judy Carne
Burt Reynolds
Tiffani-Amber Thiessen

COBO Michael Landon

COCKTAIL Edmund Lowe

COCO Liberace
Mrs. Debbie Fields
Fredric March
Evie Roberts
Sandra Bernhard
Bob Hope

COCONUT Joyce DeWitt

Joyce DeWitt has her poodle well trained. When she says the words "nose job," Coconut pushes a ball across the room with her nose.

CODY Michael Pare

COLETTE Brian Keith

COLLE King Arthur

COLONEL BLIMP
Elizabeth Taylor

COLUMBUS
Sammy Davis, Jr.

COMMISSION Clark Gable

COMTE King Charles IX

The King of France, Charles IX, was so devoted to his spaniel Comte that he let him eat off his own plate at dinner.

CONAN
Arnold Schwarzenegger

Arnold Schwarzenegger named his Labrador Retriever after the film role which made him a star, that of *Conan the Barbarian*.

Maria Shriver

CONUS Sid Caesar

Sid Caesar credits his two dogs Conus and Sascha for helping him beat his problems with alcoholism and depression.

COOKIE Mrs. Debbie Fields

COOPER Mark Harmon
Wil Shriner

COOTER Herb Albert

CORA
Edward, Duke of Windsor

When his terrier Cora became too weak to hop up on the bed, Prince Edward had steps constructed so that his pooch could join him in bed.

CORKY Jim Bakker
Tammy Faye Bakker

Tammy Faye Bakker, scandalized that her pooch Corky was having an illicit affair with a poodle named Peaches, spent over $3,000 having them properly hitched by a preacher.

Beverly Sills
Carl "Alfalfa" Switzer

CORMAC — Robin Gibb

CORNELIUS
Tennessee Williams

COTY — Ian Ziering

COUNTRY — Anson Williams

CRACKERS — King George VI

CRICKET — Betty White
Natalie Wood

CROISSANT — Loretta Swit

CRYSTAL — Dwight Clark

CUB — John James

CUBE — Brian Austin Green

CUJO — Mariette Hartley

CYCLONE — Barry Goldwater

CYRANO — Marty Ingels
Shirley Jones

D'OR — Victor Costa

Dress designer Victor Costa obtained his King Charles spaniel D'or right after signing his big contract with Christain Dior, hence the name for his pooch. D'or made his social debut at a special doggie fashion show, featuring ensembles from the exlusive Happy Tails Pet Boutique in Dallas, Texas.

DAFFODIL — Gladys, Duchess of Marlborough

DAI — David Lloyd George

DAINTY — David Cassidy

DAISEY — Marcia Rodd

DAISY
Nazimova
Tallulah Bankhead
Dagwood Bumstead
Richard Burton
Christina Crawford
Doris Day
Mariette Hartley
Dorothy Parker
Harriet Beecher Stowe
Elizabeth Taylor
E. B. White

Author E. B. White's terrier Daisy attended his wedding, but failed to stay on his best behavior. In the middle of the ceremony, he attacked the minister's dog, making a shambles of the wedding.

DAISY-JUNE — Doris Day

DAN — Dr. James Herriot

DANCER — Max Gail
Betty White

DANDELION — Jimmy Barker

DART — William Wordsworth

DAS
Winifred Barnum Newman

DASH — Benjamin Harrison
Thomas Hood
Charles Lamb
Mary Tyler Moore
Queen Victoria

The future Queen Victoria heaped luxury upon her little

friend Dash, and the first thing she did after she was crowned was rush home and give her dog a bath.

DAVIE   Woodrow Wilson

DAVY CROCKETT
    Edward, Duke of Windsor

The Duke and Duchess of Windsor were so devoted to their pugs that they supplied them with mink coats, diamond collars and 14-karat Cartier leashes. The pampered pooches enjoyed feasting on such delicacies as grilled capon breast and calves' liver, served in a silver bowl with their names engraved on the side.

DEACON   Brad Pitt

DECKEL   Queen Victoria

DELILAH   Charo

DEMI   Rock Hudson

DEREK   Patrick Swayze

DIABLO   Clara Bow

DIAMOND   King Arthur
    Bill Harris
    Sir Isaac Newton

DIANA OF WILDWOOD
    Calvin Coolidge

DICK   Wally Ford

DIDI   Kathryn Grayson

DIGBY   Shelley Duvall

DILLMAN   Jimmy Barker

DILLON   Doris Day

Doris Day is a major pet lover, and she founded the Doris Day Pet Foundation to rescue abandoned and ill-treated animals like Dillon. His former master drove him around in the back of his pick-up truck, without any restraint. Once, when the truck came to a quick stop, Dillon was thrown out and was run over by another car, losing his leg, and his owner left him in the road to die.

DINAH   Tom Sullivan
    Betty White

DING   Peggy McKay

DINKEY
    Constance Talmadge

When Constance Talmadge was the biggest star in Hollywood, and the whole world was at her feet, her favorite companion in the whole world was a little Pomeranian named Dinkey.

DINKY   Sammy Davis, Jr.

DINO   Eddie Velez

You would think that film star Eddie Velez would have his hands full with three Siberian Huskies, but he plans on eventually getting three more. He wants a full sled dog team of six Huskies so he can drive around on his trips to Alaska.

DISRAELI
Edward, Duke of Windsor

DISWILLIAM
Mary Tyler Moore

DIVEIDI
David Lloyd George

DIXIE
Mary Kate McGeehan

DJEDDA   Maria Callas
Aristotle Onassis

DOBI   Madelaine Paulson

DOC   Hubert Humphrey
Milla Jovovich

DOLL   Nancy Mitford

DOLORAS
Tallulah Bankhead

DOMINO
Olivia Newton-John

DON'T CRY   Erik Estrada

DON'T KNOW   Mark Twain

DONNA   Greg Louganis

DONNIE   Ann Sothern

DOOKIE
Queen Elizabeth II

DOPEY   Bobby Sherman

DORARICH BUTCH
Humphrey Bogart

DORIS   Michael Learned

DOS   Mrs. Debbie Fields

DOTTIE   H. R. Haldeman

DR. SAM   Sammy Davis, Jr.

DRAGEE   Gladys, Duchess
of Marlborough

DRAGO   Charlton Heston

DRIFTER   Joan Embery

DROMAS   Actaeon

DROOPY   Lauren Bacall
Humphrey Bogart

DRUJOK   Anna Sten

DUANE   Barry Gibb

DUBLIN   David Soul

DUCHESS   Jimmy Barker
Walt Disney

DUCK   Isak Dinesen

DUDLEY   Mary Tyler Moore

DUFFER   Eugene Roche

DUFFY
Franklin Delano Roosevelt

DUKE   Jimmy Barker
Joan Bennett
Clara Bow
Barbara Cartland
Elly May Clampett
Mike Douglas
Nell Shipman
John Wayne
Robin Williams

DUMPLING
Lyndon Johnson

DUSHOK   Anna Sten

DUSTY   Michael Keaton

DUTCHESS
   Franklin Delano Roosevelt

DYLAN   Sally Kellerman

EAGLEHURST GILLETTE
           Herbert Hoover

EASY   Max Gail

ECLAIR   Janine Turner

ED   Courtney Thorne-Smith

EDDIE   Judy Garland
            Sally Struthers

EDGAR   Lyndon Johnson

EDWARD   Ida Lupino

E'EN SO   Richard Burton
         Elizabeth Taylor

EIKO VON BLUTENBERG
          Dorothy Parker

ELFIE   Shannen Doherty

ELMER   Buster Keaton

EL TIGRE   Doris Day

ELSA   Elizabeth Taylor

Elizabeth Taylor was so devoted to her Lhasa Apsos, that she refused to subject them to Britain's six-month quarantine on foreign animals while she was shooting a film. To keep them with her, she rented a yacht and moored it in the Thames River, perhaps the most expensive kennel in history, so that she could sleep with them every night.

ELVIS   Jack Wagner

EMILY   Peggy Guggenheim

EMMA   Allen Ludden

Allen Ludden knew that his children, David, Martha, and Sarah, were very upset over the death of their mother, so he brought into their lives two miniature chocolate poodles, Willie and Emma, knowing that animals would help to heal their pain.

              Betty White

EMPRESS   Jimmy Barker

ENGELBERT
   General George S. Patton

ERDA   Maurice Sendak

EROS   Prince Albert

E.T.   Gene Roddenberry

ETHEL   Ronnie Schell

EVALITA   Beverly D'Angelo

EVE   Anthony Edwards

EXPLORER
   Albert Payson Terhune

EZRA POUND
        F. Scott Fitzgerald
          Zelda Fitzgerald

FAIR ELLEN
   Albert Payson Terhune

FAITHFUL
   Ulysses Simpson Grant

FAL
   Franklin Delano Roosevelt

FALLON   John Forsythe

John Forsythe, who played Blake Carrington on the long-running prime time soap series *Dynasty*, named his two toy poodles after the names of the characters of his wife Krystle Carrington and his daughter Fallon Carrington on the series.

FAMOUS   Audrey Hepburn

Audrey Hepburn's Yorkie had such a nervous disposition, he couldn't even cross a road without the support of his own personal tranquilizer pills.

FANG   Joan Fontaine

FANNIE   Earl Holliman

FANNY   Grace Kelly
     Prince Rainier of Monaco

FARLEY   Earl Holliman

FATTY   Staci Keanan

FAUNU
   Elizabeth Barrett Browning

FAWN HALL   Dennis Quaid

Dennis Quaid called his Golden Retriever Fawn Hall because she shreds everything.

FEATHER   Marcia Rodd

FEETS   Lawrence Sanders

FELLER   Harry S. Truman

FERDINAND   Peggy McKay

FERDINANDO
     Ingrid Bergman
     Isabella Rossellini

When she was a little girl, Isabella Rossellini had to have her spine surgically straightened to prevent her from becoming a hunchback. While she was in a body cast for two years, her faithful pet Ferdinando never left her side.

FERN   Carol Burnett

FIDO   Abraham Lincoln

Abraham Lincoln went down in history when he named his dog Fido, which ever since has vied with George Washington's dog Rover as the most popular name for a canine companion. Unfortunately, Fido was also assassinated, stabbed to death by a frightened drunk.

FIFI   Jill St. John
     Robert Wagner

FIGARO   Kay Johnson

FIONA   Richard Condon

FLANNEL   Stephen Crane

FLEA BAILEY   Lia Belli

FLIC   Dorothy Parker

FLIP   Gregory Peck

FLORA   Edward Lear

FLORENCE Gary Collins
Mary Ann Mobley

FLOSSY Anne Bronte

FLOYD Harry Anderson

FLUFF Katherine Cornell

FLUFFY Queen Victoria

FLUSH
Elizabeth Barrett Browning

The poetess Elizabeth Barrett Browning was not allowed by her tyrannical father to have any friends, so she got a little red cocker spaniel. She finally outwitted her father and found a husband, but by that time she was so attached to her little dog that she refused to go on her honeymoon without him.

Robert Browning

FLY Sarah Bernhardt
Beatrix Potter

FORESTER
George Washington

FOUND Jean Howard

FOXHUGH Elvis Presley

FOXY Calvin Coolidge

FRANCIS Eddie Furlong

FRANK Mark Harmon

FRANKIE Paul Reiser

FRECKLES Lyndon Johnson
Robert F. Kennedy
Kate Smith

FRED William F. Buckley, Jr.
E. B. White

FREEBO Ronald Reagan

FREEWAY Leslie Charleson

Leslie Charleson, star of *General Hospital*, named her cocker spaniel Freeway because he is forced to spend a lot of time on the highway going back and forth to the studio.

Greg Louganis
Robert Wagner

FREYA Vita Sackville-West

FRISKEY Spiro Agnew

FRISKY Gary Collins
Mary Ann Mobley

FRITZIE William Powell

FROSTY Pat Boone
Madelaine Paulson

FUJI Donny Osmond

The Japanese government gave Donny Osmond an Akita named Fuji who turned out to be a holy terror. He bit neighbors, fought with other dogs, chased sheep and even killed a cow! It got so bad that the state of Utah declared Fuji a dangerous animal, and ordered him out of the state!

Marie Osmond
Byron Scott

FULLER Vivian Wu

FUSSY   Ellen Terry

FUZZY   Ronald Reagan

G. BOY   J. Edgar Hoover

GABY   Glenn Close
                 Louise Sorel

GANGSTER
                 Sylvester Stallone

When Sylvester Stallone travels, his dogs are never far away, and he always purchases two first class tickets for each dog, so they can travel comfortably alongside him wherever he goes.

GATCHINA
                 Alexander III of Russia

GATSBY   Julia Roberts

GEE GEE   Elizabeth Taylor
                 Michael Wilding

GEECHIE DAN   Warren G.

GEIST   Matthew Arnold

GEM   Teddy Roosevelt

GEMMY
                 Barbara Taylor Bradford

GENERAL POMPEY
                 Charlton Heston

GENGHIS KHAN
                 Zsa Zsa Gabor

GEOFFREY
                 Alfred Hitchcock

In his film *The Birds*, Hitchcock made his traditional cameo appearance with a switch: he showed up with his pet Sealyham terriers, Stanley and Geoffrey. He was so devoted to his dogs that he named his production company, "Shamley Productions," which is an anagram of Sealyham.

His Shamley Productions logo should be familiar to all devotees of his long running TV series *Alfred Hitchcock Presents*.

GEORGE   Ronald Colman
                 John Gardner
                 Melissa Gilbert
                 Michael Gray
                 Earl Holliman
                 Courtney Thorne-Smith

Courtney Thorne-Smith is a spokesperson and driving force behind PAWS (Pets Are Wonderful Support), a non-profit organization that helps people living with HIV/AIDS to keep and care for their pets. PAWS helps them care for their animals by providing pet-care services, such as walking, grooming and feeding, as well as helping with veterinary bills, and then finds foster homes for their little friends when the need arises.

GEORGE BRANDT
                 Janet Leigh

GEORGIA   Richard Burton

GERLAND	King Arthur
GERLERT	King Arthur
GIALLO	
	Walter Savage Landor
GIGI	Mary Kay Ash

Mary Kay Ash, the founder of Mary Kay Cosmetics, insists that her dog Gigi use only her products, right down to her perfectly clipped and lacquered pink toenails.

	Dr. Jane Goodall
	Beverly Sills
	Tennessee Williams

Tennessee Williams refused to be parted from his dog, and whenever he traveled, Gigi would have a first class seat right next to his own.

GILBY	Bob Hope
GILDA	Queen Victoria
GILLIE	Saki
GIN	Brigitte Bardot
GINGER	Lucille Ball
	Quinn Cummings
	Lorne Greene
	Gene Kelly
GINGER BOY	
	General Omar Bradley
GINNIE	
	George Armstrong Custer
GIORGIO	Linda Gray
GISMO	Corey Feldman

GLEN	Herbert Hoover
GOALIE	
	Mayor Rudolph Giuliani
GOGO	Greer Garson
GOLDEN BLACKIE	
	Vincent Price
GOLDIE	Vincent Price
GOOFY	Bobby Sherman
GOOGY	Eva Gabor
GORBY	Victoria Principal
GRACIE	Melissa Gilbert
GRAY DAWN	
	Albert Payson Terhune
GRETEL	Liberace
GRIGGS	Paul Newman
	Joanne Woodward
GRIM	Rutherford B. Hayes
GRIP	Wes Craven
GRITS	Amy Carter
GROCK	David Lloyd George
GROVER	Earl Holliman
GRUNK	Dinah Shore
GUAPA	Brigitte Bardot
	Deborah Kerr
GUCCI	James Hampton
GUNN	Bo Derek
GUS	Robert Duvall

Robert Duvall's favorite role was that of Gus McCrae in the miniseries *Lonesome Dove*, and it was after him that Duvall named his dog Gus.

Kelly Emberg

GWEN   King Edward VIII
Edward, Duke of Windsor

GYPSY   Suzanne Pleshette

HAILEY   Sally Struthers

HAMISH   King Edward VII
Woodrow Wilson

HAMLET   Sarah Bernhardt
Sir Walter Scott

HAMLET II   Hayley Mills

HANDSOME

Penny Marshall

HANNAH MORGANA

Edie Adams

HANS   Dorothy Eustis

HANSIE   Vincent Price

HAPPY   David Cassidy
King George V
Vincent Price

When Vincent Price was in high school, he inherited Happy, a Boston Bull terrier, from his sister. Vincent enjoyed dressing her up in costumes, which included skirts and dime store earrings, to portray such characters as Cleopatra or Mary, Queen of Scots, in the theatrical extravaganzas he staged in his room.

HAROUN

Rudolph Valentino

HARRY   Bo Derek
Paul Newman
Joanne Woodward

HARUM SCARUM   Bo Derek

HARVEY   Lauren Bacall
Humphrey Bogart

"Harvey" had been Bogie's nickname for Lauren Bacall while they were dating, named after the invisible rabbit in the play *Harvey*. This was because Bogie was still married, and Bacall had to be invisible. When they received a boxer as a wedding present, the name was a natural for their new pet.

Prince Charles

HASI   Elke Sommer

HAZBER   Joan Fontaine

HEATHCLIFF   June Allyson

June Allyson didn't name her pet after the comic strip cat, she went right to the source and named him after the hero in her favorite movie, *Wuthering Heights*.

Dick Powell

HEATHER   King George V

HECTOR   Dr. James Herriot
Bela Lugosi

HEIDI   Pat Boone
Dwight D. Eisenhower
Charlton Heston

Earle Jorgensen
Jimmy McNichol
Emma Samms
William Shatner

HEINEKEN   Doris Day

HELEN
    William Randolph Hearst

Helen, a dachshund, was William Randolph Hearst's closest companion for over fifteen years. She was buried with great ceremony at San Simeon, his mansion, under a tombstone that reads "Here lies dearest Helen, my devoted friend. W.R.H."

HELP AND HAND
        King Robert the Bruce

HENESSEY   Warren G.

HENRIETTA
            Richard Thomas

HENRY   Demi Moore

Demi Moore spares no expense where her pampered pooches are concerned, right down to the $400 booties that she purchased for her Yorkie Henry.

                    Bruce Willis

HEPHASTIAN   Peter Lapis

HER   Lyndon Johnson

HERBIE   DeAnna Robbins

HERO   Bo Derek

HIM   Lyndon Johnson

HITCHCOCK
        Tallulah Bankhead

Alfred Hitchcock gave Tallulah Bankhead a Sealingham while directing her in *Lifeboat*, which she promptly dubbed Hitchcock.

HOBO   Chuck Eisenmann

HOGAN   David Kelley

HOLLY
    Admiral Richard E. Byrd

HOMER   Rex Harrison

HONDO   Dan Reeves

HONEY   Prince Charles
            Doris Day
        Queen Elizabeth II
            Priscilla Presley

HONEY BEAR
        Susan Saint James

HONEY PIE
        Susan Richardson

HOOPLA   Helen Hayes

HOOVER   Burt Bacharach

HUB   Warren G. Harding

HUGHIE   Rick Wallace

HUGO   Arthur Miller
            Marilyn Monroe

When Marilyn Monroe was getting her divorce from playwright Arthur Miller, she tried to get custody of Hugo, but it was Miller who walked away from the marriage with the basset hound.

Anna Lee Nathan

HYLACTOR — Actaeon

I KNOW — Mark Twain

IGLOO — Admiral Richard E. Byrd

IGOR — Laraine Day

IMAN — Czar Nicholas II

INGA — Billy Wilder

INGO — Catherine Bach

Catherine Bach is a spokeswoman for the World Wildlife Fund. She addressed the Senate on behalf of the Black Rhino and Tiger Conservation Act of 1994.

INNI — Brigitte Bardot

IO — Maurice Sendak

IRISH TERRIER — Eugene O'Neill

ISLAY — Queen Victoria

IVORY — Bo Derek

J. EDGAR — Lyndon Johnson

JACK — King Edward VII

Jack, the Irish terrier of King Edward VII, would lurk under the throne, waiting to pounce on unsuspecting victims. The King indulged him in every way, even when Jack would chomp into an ambassador or a Prime Minister.

🐾 Dog Names

King George V
Joey Lawrence
Fred MacMurray
Teddy Roosevelt

JACKIE — Gerald Ford

JACKSON — Olivia Newton-John

JACQUES — Liberace

JAGGERS — Edward, Duke of Windsor

JAGSS — Stephen Macht

Actor Stephen Macht created the name of his dog Jagss by combining the initials of everyone in his family, Julie, Jessie, Ari, Gabriel, Suzanne and Stephen.

JAGUAR — Barbara Lazaroff
Wolfgang Puck

JAKE — Dan Reeves

JAMES — Agatha Christie

JAN — Pablo Picasso

JANE — Queen Elizabeth II
King George VI

JASMINE — Ann Miller

JASON — Rex Harrison
Vivien Leigh

JASPER — John Houseman

JEANNIE — James Thurber
JENNIE — Earl Holliman
Maurice Sendak
James Thurber

JENNIFER — Bea Arthur

	John Huston
	Evelyn Keyes
	Sidney Sheldon
JENNY	David Hasselhoff
JERRY	F. Scott Fitzgerald
	Zelda Fitzgerald
	John Huston
	Evelyn Keyes
JESSAMYN	Erma Bombeck
JESSIE	Valerie Harper
	Dennis Quaid
	Teddy Roosevelt
JESTER	Ellen Sandler
JET	Robert Davenport
	Rawley Farnsworth
	Jack Youngblood
JEZEBELL	Alan Ladd
JIGGS	Louise Sorel
JIMMY	Edy Williams
JIP	Abraham Lincoln
JO-FI	Sigmund Freud

Sigmund Freud became very distraught at the death of his chow Jo-Fi. In remembrance, he would hum the aria from Mozart's *Don Juan*, the theme of which is friendship.

JO-JO	Liberace
JOCK	Nancy Mitford
JOCKO	Will Rogers
JOE	Cloris Leachman
	Edmund Lowe
	Vincent Price

Vincent Price has had a lot of pets, but by far his favorite was Joe. So dedicated was he to his canine buddy that he wrote a book about him, called *The Book of Joe*.

JOEY	Susan Clark
	Alex Karras
	Patricia McCormack

JOHNNY   Lionel Barrymore

During World War II, the government collected scrap rubber for the war effort. Lionel Barrymore's terrier Johnny was so incensed that his rubber toys were confiscated, that he wrote a letter of complaint to FDR's dog Fala.

	Queen Elizabeth II
	Vincent Price
JOHNSON	Dwight Clark
	Bob Goen
JOKER	Don Rickles

JOLLY JANE
            Calvin Coolidge

JONES	E. B. White
JONESEY	Jack Jones
JOSEPH	Tom Cruise
	Jacqueline Susann

JOSEPHINE
            Jacqueline Susann

JOY
   Alexis, Tsarevich of Russia

| JUAN | Bob Barker |

JUBILEE MORN
        Duke of Marlborough

JUDA   Stephen Macht

JUDGE   James Thurber

JULIE   John Gavin
                S. J. Perelman
                James Thurber
                Nathanael West

JULIUS   Sid Caesar

JUNIOR   Lucille Ball
                Demi Moore
                Maureen O'Sullivan
                Bruce Willis

JUPITER   Jimmy Cannon

KABAR   Rudolph Valentino

Rudolph Valentino's dog Kabar was the first pet buried in the Los Angeles Pet Park.

KABUL   Pablo Picasso

KACHINA   Max Ernst
                Peggy Guggenheim

KAISER   Matthew Arnold

KAMIKAZE   Helen Keller

In 1937, Helen Keller became the first person to bring an Akita into the United States from Japan. With the onslaught of World War II, Helen came to regret the name Kamikaze (divine wind) when Kamikaze dive bombers began sinking American fighting ships.

KARL   Norman Mailer

KARMA   DeAnna Robbins

KARTY   Lorenzo Lamas

KATE   Bill Blass
                King Edward VIII
        Edward, Duke of Windsor

KATIE   Richard Basehart
                Susan Dey
                Earl Holliman

KATO
        Nicole Brown Simpson

KEEPER   Emily Bronte

When Emily Bronte died, her mastiff Keeper followed the funeral procession and then slept for weeks after her death at the door of her empty room.

                Mai Zetterling

KELLY   Jean Kerr

KENO   Jane Ardmore
                Lee Purcell

KENZAN GO   Helen Keller

KEP   Beatrix Potter

KIDDO   Susan Saint James

KIKI   Kathryn Grayson
                Orson Welles

KILLER   Bo Derek
                David Hasselhoff
                Debbie Reynolds
                Tammy Wynette

KILLER DOG
        Martina Navratilova

KILLIE   T. H. White

KILTIE   Caspar Weinberger

KIM   Lyndon Johnson

KIMBERLY
                Earl of Mountbatten

KING   Jimmy Barker
                    Jimmy Durante
                    Lorne Greene

KINGA   Blair Underwood

Blair Underwood was brought up in Germany as an "Army brat," and was able to easily master the German commands he needed to control his German Shepherds—although they pretend not to understand the word "nein."

KING ARTHUR
                Adlai Stevenson

KING KOLE   Calvin Coolidge

KING KONG
                Marisa Berenson

KING TIMAHOE
                Richard Nixon

KING TUT   Herbert Hoover

KIRK   William Shatner

William Shatner named his Doberman after his most famous role, that of Captain Kirk. When the dog became ill, Shatner took him to see Beatrice Lydecker, who, after a Vulcan mind meld with the pooch, discovered that his back was hurt when his crate had been dropped in shipment. After some acupuncture, he had been totally cured.

KIS LANY   Eva Gabor
                    Zsa Zsa Gabor

KITTY   Mrs. Debbie Fields

KLEINE   Arte Johnson

KNOCKWURST
                Rita Hayworth

KNUDLE   Arte Johnson

KRIS   Karl Lewis Miller

KRONEN   Ruta Lee

KRYPTO   Superman

Another survivor of the doomed planet Krypton, Superman's dog Krypto had all of his powers, plus super smell, which allowed him to sniff out criminals.

KRYSTLE   John Forsythe

LABROS   Actaeon

LACHNE   Actaeon

LACY   Sean Young

LAD   Albert Payson Terhune

LADADOG   Jean Kerr

LADDIE   Lou Costello
                    Nell Shipman
                    Queen Victoria

LADDIE BOY
                Warren G. Harding

Laddie Boy was not only one of the most popular of White House pets, but also the most opinionated. He regularly gave interviews to the *Washington Post* on political topics, and took a firm stand on an eight-hour work day for guard dogs. Laddie Boy had his own special seat in the cabinet, and his own social secretary to keep his appointment calendar.

LADDIE BUCK
Calvin Coolidge
Woodrow Wilson

LADY   Jimmy Barker
Sheena Easton
Earl Holliman
Jerry Lewis
Donny Osmond
Tyrone Power
Ronald Reagan
Albert Payson Terhune
George Washington

LADY ASHLEY   Eva Gabor

LADY BUG   Sylvia Sidney

LADY DI   Liberace

LADY II   Donny Osmond

LADY III   Donny Osmond

LAMBCHOP   Greg Louganis

LAMPON   King Midas

LANCE   Robert Goulet
Carol Lawrence

LARA   James Buchanan

LASSIE   Lou Costello

LAURA   Princess Anne

LAVERNE   Michael Landon
Louise Shaffer

LAZLO   Susan Clark
Alex Karras

LEADER   Senator Bob Dole

Senator Bob Dole's miniature schnauzer Leader is named after his position as the Senate Majority Leader. Leader has been known to sneak down to the Capitol rotunda and bark at the Senators there, but he only attacks the liberal ones.

LEASEL   Rick Springfield

LEBBO   Anna Pavlova

LEBROS   Actaeon

LELAPS   Actaeon

LEROY BROWN
Frank Sinatra

LETHAL RON
Rick Springfield

LEUCITE   Actaeon

LIBERTY   Gerald Ford

LICKETY SPITZ
Dolly Parton

LIDO   Madelaine Paulson

LILAC   Rita Hayworth

LILINE   King Charles IX

LILLIE   Cheech Marin

LILLY   Robert Lynch
Liza Minnelli

Liza Minnelli's cairn terrier Lilly became a tabloid star herself when she was barred from accompanying Liza to Sweden because of their quarantine laws. With Lilly exiled to Paris, Liza became totally distraught over their first separation.

LILY LANGTRY
    Eleanor "Cissy" Patterson

LINCOLN   Stephen Dorff

LINUS   Garry Marshall

LION   King Arthur

LISA   Vincent Price
    Darryl Zanuck

In Darryl Zanuck's retirement, his two Yorkies Lisa and Tina were his closest companions. In his will, he bequeathed them to his wife Virginia.

LITTLE BEAGLE
    Lyndon Johnson

LITTLE CHAP
    Lyndon Johnson

LOBO   Joseph Jackson

Joseph Jackson, the father of Michael, Janet, and LaToya, became paranoid after Charlie Manson's murder of actress Sharon Tate, and bought a guard dog named Lobo to look after his talented brood.

LOCHINVAR BOBBY
    Bobby Sherman

LOCH LOMMOND
    Bo Derek

LOKI   Gary Collins
    Jared Martin
    Mary Ann Mobley

LOLA   Colette

LONDON
    Chuck Eisenmann

LOOTY   Queen Victoria

The Pekingese breed was restricted to the royal family of China until the British army took Peking in 1860. Amid the dead bodies of the royal family were found Pekingese, which were promptly sent back to Queen Victoria. She named her favorite Looty because he was the "loot" of their victory over China.

LORD BUTTON
    Beatrice Little

LOTTIE   Nancy Mitford

LOVE   Mike Douglas

LOWEY
    William F. Buckley, Jr.

LUATH   King Arthur

LU-LU   Marty Ingels
    Shirley Jones

LUCILLE   Dick Clark

LUCKY   Clyde Beatty

Ava Gardner
Paul Newman
Al Pacino
Ronald Reagan

LUCY
Thom Bray
Mike Douglas
Michael Landon
Garry Marshall
Ronnie Schell
Tanya Tucker

LUCY BROWN
Red Buttons

LUFFRA   King Arthur

LUKE   Merle Oberon

LULU   Kristy McNichol
Francoise Sagan
Queen Victoria
Roger & Louise Williams
Mike Winters

LUMP   Pablo Picasso

Convinced that his mutt Lump, being a city dog, had never seen a rabbit, Picasso painted one on a cardboard cutout. Lump immediately atacked and ate the pseudo bunny, becoming the only one to ever eat an original Picasso.

LUNCHEON TOM
Nancy Mitford

LUNYU   Sigmund Freud

LUPE   Bob Barker

LUSKA   King Edward VII

LYCISA   Actaeon

LYLE   Cornelia Guest

MAC   E. B. White

MACBARKER   Gina Gallego
Mr. Magoo

MACHITO   Evelyn Keyes
Artie Shaw

MACHO   Brigitte Bardot
Zsa Zsa Gabor

MACKIE
Gertrude Lawrence

MADAME MOOSE
George Washington

MADAME SOPHIA
Tennessee Williams

MADELEINE
Sally Jessy Raphael

MADISON   Tomie De Paola
Demi Moore
Bruce Willis

MAF   Arthur Miller
Marilyn Monroe

When Marilyn received a French poodle from Frank Sinatra, she called him Mafia, and then later shortened it to Maf.

MAGGIE
Melissa Sue Anderson
Michael Gray
Dustin Hoffman
Earl Holliman
Bob Waterfield

MAGILLACUDDY
Maureen McGovern

Singer Maureen McGovern's dog Magillacuddy knows and loves his master's singing. Whenever he hears her singing *The Morning After* on the radio, he sits up and gets excited.

MAGNOLIA
Tallulah Bankhead
Tony Dow

MAIDA
George Armstrong Custer
Sir Walter Scott

MAJOR Irene Dunne
Patricia Ellis
Franklin Delano Roosevelt

MAJOR HOMER Q. PUTNAM
Cecil B. DeMille
William DeMille

Film director brothers Cecil B. DeMille and William DeMille named their childhood dog after Major Homer Q. Putnam, a character in one of their father's plays.

MAKEBA
Malcolm-Jamal Warner

Malcolm-Jamal Warner came up with a unique way to fix the alarm system in his Toyota Land Cruiser when it broke down. He replaced that system with his dogs Mecca and Makeba, who ride around in the truck with him. An unexpected advantage is that he can aways leave the windows down, so he doesn't come back to a hot truck!

MANCHU Teddy Roosevelt

MAN FRIDAY Errol Flynn

MANNIE Jimmy Barker
Earl Holliman

MARCO Queen Victoria

MARCO POLO
Douglas Fairbanks

MARIKO Kate Vernon

MARIPOSA Elizabeth Taylor

MARKSMAN
Franklin Delano Roosevelt

MARK SPITZ Dolly Parton

MARLBOROUGH
Jimmy Barker

MARMADUKE
Melody Rogers

MARTHA Paul McCartney

MARTIKA William Shatner

MARTINI Cheryl Tiegs

MARTY WIENER
Richard Simmons

MARY Michael Landon

MARY ELIZABETH
Elinor Donahue

MAS Lorenzo Lamas

MATEJ Milos Forman

MATHE King Richard II

Not all dogs are loyal. When Richard II lost his throne and was sent to prison, his greyhound Mathe promptly transferred his loyalty to the new king.

MATT	James Arness

James Arness, the star of the long-running television series *Gunsmoke*, named his two Bichon Frises after characters in his show, one for his own role, that of Marshall Matt Dillon, and the other for his leading lady, Miss Kitty.

MAUD	Jimmy Barker

Gallery owner Jimmy Barker tours in a van so that all 23 of his Cavalier King Charles spaniels can travel with him at the same time.

MAUDE	Mary Tyler Moore
MAX	Don Adams
	Matthew Arnold
	Steffi Graf
	Deidre Hall
	John Larroquette
	Brian Mitchell
	George C. Scott
	Sidney Sheldon
	Martha Stewart
	Scott Weinger
	Bionic Woman
MAXIMILLIAN	Louise Shaffer
MAYBELLINE	Dick Clark

Dick Clark's offices, even though they are right across the street from NBC, are so informal that dogs are allowed to roam freely from office to office. And Maybelline is the most mobile. She waits for someone to push the button on the elevator, and then rides from floor to floor, personally helping Dick Clark run his music and TV empire.

MCCORMICK	Jonathan Taylor Thomas
MECCA	Malcolm-Jamal Warner
ME-TOO	Stewart Granger
	Jean Simmons
MEDVE	James Thurber
MEENY	Kathryn Grayson
MEG	Bette Davis
MEGAN	Jonathan Brandis
MEGGIE	Eleanor Roosevelt
	Franklin Delano Roosevelt
MELAMPUS	Actaeon
MELANEUS	Actaeon
MELANIE	Richard Simmons
MELON	Barbara Lazaroff
	Wolfgang Puck
MERLE	Emma Samms
MERLIN	Bert Lahr

Bert Lahr, who played the Cowardly Lion in the *Wizard of Oz*, loved Toto so much he decided he had to have his own cairn terrier, Merlin.

Adlai Stevenson

MERRY   John Lennon
             Sean Lennon
             Yoko Ono

MICA   Katharine Hepburn

MICHAEL MOO   Linda Gray

MIDNIGHT   Dom DeLuise
             Tyra Banks

MIIKO   Hal Williams

MIKA   Pia Zadora

MIKE   Nazimova
             Miriam Cooper
             Bob Hope
             Harry S. Truman

MIKIE   Michael Landon

MILES   Marty Ingels

MILLIE   George Bush

Millie, the First Dog of President Bush, published her memoirs, *Millie's Book*, becoming the first dog to have a book on the best-seller list.

             Nancy Mitford
             Ronald Reagan

MIMSY   King George VI

MIN   Henry David Thoreau

MING   Michael York

MINICCIO   Sarah Bernhardt

MINK   Rita Hayworth

MINKA   Dudley Moore

MINNIE   Karen Black
             Sylvia Fairbanks

Clark Gable
Anjelica Huston

MINUET   Liberace

MISCHI   Liberace

MISHKA   Zsa Zsa Gabor
             Harris Katleman

MISS BRINDA
             Tennessee Williams

Tennessee Williams' favorite pet was his dog Miss Brinda, who had every possible defect including walleyes and practically no legs. All of her medical problems notwithstanding, she actually used to pose with the fashion models in Rome at the foot of the Spanish Steps, but never for longer than one hour at a time.

MISS KITTY   James Arness

MISS MAGOO   Eva Gabor
                Miss Mouse
                Carol Lawrence

MISS WIGGLES
                Frank Sinatra

MISSY   Claudette Colbert
             Janet Gaynor

MISTER STUBBS
                Robert Reed

MISTY   Gerald Ford
                Dorothy Parker

When author Dorothy Parker was being interviewed by the FBI in 1951 for being a subversive, Misty kept jumping up on the agents. Finally, Dorothy said, "Listen, I can't even get my dog to stay down. Do I look to you like someone who could overthrow the government?"

MITZI   Mr. Rogers
                         George Hamilton

George Hamilton appeared on an episode of Cybill Shepherd's sitcom *Cybill* with his Yorkie Mitzi in tow. An intergral part of the plot, Mitzi obligingly leaves a little poo-poo on the ground, which is promptly scooped up by Cybill. She puts it into a paper bag, puts it on a friend's porch, lights it on fire, rings the bell, and then laughs hysterically when he tries to stomp it out.

MIZA   Edith Wharton

MOCHA   Dean Cain

MOE   John F. Kennedy

MOKA   Diana Barrymore

MOLLY   Dick Clark
                         Bo Derek
                         Deidre Hall

MONA   Richard Condon

MONCHE   Brigitte Bardot

MONY   Rudy Vallee

MOOGIE   Linda Blair

MOONBEAM
                    David L. Wolper

MOOSE   Kathryn Grayson

MOP   Queen Victoria

MOPSEY
               George Washington

MORGAN   Ava Gardner

MORITZ   Basil Rathbone

Basil Rathbone's sheepdog Moritz was also a celebrity, as the spokesdog in advertisements for Calvert Reserve Whiskey. It is not known if Basil let him keep the royalties.

MOSS   Thomas Hardy

MOUJIK   Yves St. Laurent

Yves St. Laurent makes his dog Moujik work for a living—as a model at fashion shows. He is also pampered, however, and even had his portrait painted by Andy Warhol.

MR. DEEDS   Fay Wray

MR. KELLY   Rod McKuen

MR. MOON
                Tennessee Williams

MR. PET   Nat King Cole
                        Natalie Cole

MR. PUNCH
               Winston Churchill

MR. T   Jayne Meadows
                        Steve Allen

If one happens to call Steve Allen on the telephone and he's not home, his answering machine message has his springer spaniel Mr. T barking directions to the mystified caller.

MRS. BOUNCER
Charles Dickens

MRS. PEEL   Jamie Farr

MUDDY WATER
F. Scott Fitzgerald
Zelda Fitzgerald

MUFF   Duke of Kent

MUFFIN   Joanne Carson
Johnny Carson
Ronald Reagan
Aaron Spelling
Tori Spelling

Tori Spelling is just crazy about her little dog Muffin, and when he started losing his teeth, she thought nothing about having him fitted with dentures so that he could continue to chomp on his food.

MUFFY   Doris Day
Uma Thurman

MUGGS   James Thurber

MUGGSIE   Marilyn Monroe

MUGSY   Jay Osmond

MULE EARS
Calvin Coolidge

MUMSHAY   June Havoc
Gypsy Rose Lee

MUSIC William Wordsworth

MUTT   E. B. White

NABISCO   Henry Kravis

What pooch wouldn't be jealous of Henry Kravis' Nabisco? Kravis heads the Nabisco empire, and as such has unlimited access to a variety of products, including Milkbone dog biscuits.

NADIA   Leif Garrett

NANA   Wendy Darling
Serge Gainsbourg

NANCY   Dom DeLuise

NASTASHA   Julie Parrish

NATASHA   Flip Wilson

NATO
General George C. Marshall

NEGUS   Eva Braun
Adolf Hitler

Adolf Hitler was devoted to Eva Braun's scotties Negus and Stasi, but was afraid to be seen with them because they were not in keeping with his Aryan image. Therefore, he preferred to have his picture taken with his Alsatian Blondi.

NEIL
George & Marion Kerby

While Neil the St. Bernard actually belonged to George and Marion Kerby, who were ghosts, it was actually Cosmo Topper, their reluctant host, who was inconvenienced, since liquor bottles were always missing from Cosmo's bar whenever Neil was around.

NELL	Richard Basehart
NERO	Paul Bunyan
NICK	Devon Gummersall Jerome Robbins
NICKY	Allen Ludden Maureen McGovern
NIELSEN	Bill Kirchenbauer

Bill Kirchenbauer, star of TV's *Just the Ten of Us*, named his dog Nielsen in the hopes that it would bring him luck in the real Nielsen ratings.

NIKKI	James Garner
NIMROD	Sir Walter Scott
NINI	Brigitte Bardot
NINO	Queen Victoria
NIP	Beatrix Potter
NIPPER	Melody Rogers
NIPPER DOG	
	Mary McDonough
NITRO	Jack Scalia

Jack Scalia, macho star of *Dallas*, is still glad to have the protection of his two powerful Rottweilers, Nitro and Tara, who have twice saved him from being mugged.

NOEL	Liberace
NOGI	Dorothy Parker
NONNE	King Louis XIV
NOOFY	Burt Bacharach
NOOVER	
	Carole Bayer Sager
NUGGET	Eydie Gorme Steve Lawrence
NUISANCE	Alexander Korda
NUTMEG	Della Reese
ODIN	Carol Lawrence
ODYSSEUS	Liz Smith
OH BOY	Warren G. Harding Woodrow Wilson
OLIVER	Jimmy Barker Chick Hearn Grace Kelly Prince Rainier of Monaco
OLIVIA	Wallis Annenberg
OREO	Jonathan Prince
ORIGINAL GANGSTER	
	Warren G.
ORTHROSE	King Arthur
OSCAR	Jean Harlow Howard Koch, Sr. Katie Wagner Natalie Wood
OSCEOLA	Isak Dinesen
OSHKOSH	Calvin Coolidge
OSSIE	Donny Osmond
OTHELLO	Virginia Woolf
PABLO	Vincent Price
PACHYTUS	Actaeon
PADDY	Mark Harmon

PADEREWSKI   Vincent Price

PALO ALTO
                Calvin Coolidge

PAMPER   Bo Derek

PANACHE   Mary Frann

Mary Frann had a terrible time naming her dog, so she had a "name-the-dog" dinner party. When that didn't work, she had a "name-the-dog contest" on the set of her TV show *Newhart*, where the pooch was well known, and this finally resulted in the name Panache.

PANDA   Bijan
                Kathryn Grayson
                   Hugh O'Brian
                   Vincent Price

PANDY   Vincent Price

PANSY   Ray Aghayan
                   Bob Mackie
                   Vincent Price

PAPPILLON
            Mrs. Debbie Fields

PAPPY   Dorothy Lee

PARIS   Brian Keith
                William Shatner

PARK BARBARIAN
                Ronald Colman

PASHA   Tricia Nixon

PASOP   Isak Dinesen

PASQUATE   Vincent Price

PAT   Miriam Cooper

                Herbert Hoover

PATAPON   Brigitte Bardot

PATCHES   Nichelle Nichols

PATI   Colette

PATIENCE   Vincent Price

PATRICK   Merv Griffin
                Herbert Hoover
                   Princess Mary

PATTY   Dick Martin

PAUL   King Edward VII

PAUL PRY   Calvin Coolidge

PEACHES   Jim Bakker
            Tammy Faye Bakker

PEANUT   Bo Derek

PECHICHO   W. H. Hudson

PECOSA   Luci Johnson

PEE-WEE   Elizabeth Taylor

PEEDEE   Jack Jones

PEGGY   King Edward VII
                   Ronald Reagan
      Franklin Delano Roosevelt

PENELOPE   Vincent Price

PENNY   Audrey Hepburn
                   Natalie Wood

PEPE   Bob Barker
            Yvonne De Carlo
                   Cole Porter
                   Gertrude Stein

PEPPER   David Cassidy
            William Christopher
            Christina Crawford
                   Isak Dinesen

46

Author Isak Dinesen named her dog after the Pepper in the works of Sir Walter Scott, the author who actually named the breed when he called them Danie Dinmont's in his book *Guy Mannering*.

Merle Haggard
Aaron Spelling

Aaron Spelling has a house full of dogs, and Pepper, a New Zealand Terrier, came into their house as a gift from Ricardo Montalban after the dog's short career on *Fantasy Island*.

PEPPY   Michael Gray

PERCIVAL   Vincent Price

PERCY   Victoria Wyndham

PERITES
            Alexander the Great

PERRY   Gregory Peck

PET   Liv Ullmann

PETE   Teddy Roosevelt

Teddy Roosevelt let his menagerie of animals run rampant around the White House. Pete once went after the French Ambassador Jusseraud, who barely escaped, with pieces of his trousers left scattered behind to mark his stay at the Executive Mansion.

Debra Winger

PETER   Agatha Christie

Agatha Christie was known to dedicate her books to the "O.F.D.," her code for "The Order of Faithful Dogs," which included her faithful terrier Peter.

King Edward VII
Katharine Hepburn

PETER PAN Calvin Coolidge

PETEY   Wil Shriner
Sylvia Sidney
Halle Berry

Halle Berry, co-star with Eddie Murphy in *Boomerang*, had a pet Maltese dog Bumper. When she thought Bumper was getting depressed, her vet gave her the idea to buy a little puppy Petey and hide him in the house where Bumper could find him and think he was his. The idea worked, Bumper quickly took to the little fellow, and now she has two dogs. She goes everywhere with her little friends, even grocery shopping, where they ride in the cart and help her decide what to buy.

PETIE   Little Rascals

PHANTOM   Rex Harrison
David Niven

When David Niven received a boxer as a present from friends, he named it Phantom, after the commando unit he commanded in World War II. He waded ashore the first day at Normandy, and the unit operated from D-Day until the fall of Berlin, gathering intelligence on German operations for the top brass.

PHEARLESS	Phyllis Diller
PHOEBE	King Arthur
	Carol Burnett
PICAYUNE	Vincent Price
PICCOLO	Anais Nin
PICHNON	Brigitte Bardot
PIERRE	Miriam Cooper
PIG PAW	Jimmy Barker
PILSNER	Linda Blair
PINKER	Virginia Woolf
PINKIE	Tom Mix
PINTO	Earl Holliman
	Vincent Price
PIP	Donny Osmond
	Robert Vaughn
PIPPIN	Joy Adamson
PITTY PAT	
	Richard Simmons
PIXIE	Maria Callas
	Aristotle Onassis
PLEASURE	Princess Anne
PLEDGE	Keenan Wynn
PLUTO	John Larroquette
	Mickey Mouse

	Craig T. Nelson
POACHER	Earl Holliman
POCKETS	Kaye Ballard
POEMENIS	Actaeon
POKER	Sheena Easton
POMERO	
	Walter Savage Landor
PONCHO	Shirley Temple
PONGO	Anne Bancroft
	Mary Hayley Bell
	Mel Brooks
PONNE	King Louis XIV
POO	Gloria Swanson
POOCHIE	Merv Griffin
	Earle Jorgensen
POOH BEAR	Joanne Carson
POOKIE	George DiCenzo
	Prince Edward
	Henry Kravis
	Stan Lee
POOKLES	Rita Hayworth
POOR POOH	Prince Charles

When Prince Charles' Jack Russell terrier disappeared, it ignited a nationwide search for the pooch. After the pet failed to turn up, one newspaper headline was not so kind, however, it said, "At Least He's Still Got His Mistress."

POPCORN	Jewel Shepard
POPEYE	P. Pruett

POPPY SEED	Jimmy Barker
POPS	Glenn Miller
PORTIA	Charlton Heston
POSSUM	Jack London

Jack London's dog was so devoted to his master that when Jack died, Possum drowned himself in grief.

POTATOES	Natalie Wood
POUCETTE	Colette
POWDER PUFF	Liberace
	Stephen Crane
	Jayne Mansfield
PRAIRIE	Axl Rose
PRECIOUS PENELOPE	
	Shannen Doherty
PREPPY	George DiCenzo
PRESIDENT	
	Franklin Delano Roosevelt
PRETZEL	Ruth Etting
PRINCE	Paul W. Fairman
	Jack Pickford
	Rudolph Valentino
	William Wordsworth
PRINCESS	Jimmy Barker
	Tyrone Power
PRISSY	Richard Simmons
PRUDENCE	Vincent Price
PRUDENCE PRIM	
	Calvin Coolidge
PRUNELLA	Liberace
PSEAN	Vincent Price

PUDDLE	Lauren Bacall
PUFF	Vida Dana
PUFFY	Janet Jackson
PUMPKIN	Mary Hart
	Ethel Kennedy
PUNKY	Kaye Ballard
	Betty Grable

Betty Grable put her pets above her career. After preparing all day for a big meeting with Sam Goldwyn to get the role of Adelaide in the film *Guys and Dolls*, in limped Punky with a foxtail burr imbedded in his paw. She rushed him to the animal hospital, and Goldwyn was so incensed at being stood up that he gave the role to Vivian Blaine.

	DeAnna Robbins
PUPI	Georgette Klinger
PUPPY	Earl Holliman
PURTY	Brad Pitt
PUSHINKA	
	Caroline Kennedy

When Pushinka arrived at the White House, a gift from Nikita Khrushchev, the secret service immediately took him to Walter Reed army hospital. There he was checked for microphones, hidden explosives and possible germ warfare. Remembering the Trojan

Horse, it is sometimes best to beware Russians bearing gifts.

Nikita Khrushchev

PUSHKA   Georgette Klinger

Georgette Klinger, who runs posh salons in the most fashionable parts of the country, including New York, Palm Beach and Beverly Hills, never leaves the house without her treasured poodle Pushka, who is carried everywhere in her own personally designed Louis Vuitton carrying case.

PUSSYCAT   Gardner McKay

QUINCE   T. H. White

QUIZZICAL
Armand Deutsch

RADLEY   Jimmy Barker

RAGS   Dorothy Parker
Tim Reid

RAJAH
Edgar Rice Burroughs

If you are mystified by the name of the publisher on some of Edgar Rice Burroughs' books, it is because Rajah is actually his pet collie.

RALPH   Sara Gilbert

RAMA   Ken Norton

RAMULLAH   Ali Khan

RANDY   Earl Holliman

RANGER   George Bush

RASTA   Doug Cristy

RAT   Gore Vidal

RAURA   Chuck Eisenmann

REBELL   Unity Mitford

RECESSION   Bob Hope

RED   Pam Dawber
Mark Harmon

RED BANDIT   Eddie Velez

RED DOG   Gary Crosby

REGGIE   Robin Riker
Elizabeth Taylor
Abe Vigoda

REGINA   Jimmy Barker

REK   Milos Forman

REMESES   Charlton Heston

REN   Barry Gibb

REX   Jimmy Barker
Michael J. Fox
Nancy Reagan
Ronald Reagan
James Thurber

RHETT BUTLER
Richard Simmons

RIELEY   Arnold Palmer

RIFF   Bruce Lee

Bruce Lee's dog Riff was the brother of Steve McQueen's schnauzer.

RIKKI TIKKI TAVI
Robert Ludlum

RIP   Sidney Zoom

RITA — Gladys, Duchess of Marlborough

ROB — Bo Derek

ROB ROY — Calvin Coolidge

ROBIN — Peggy Guggenheim

ROBINSON — Dorothy Parker

ROCCO — Bernadette Peters

ROCKET — Ed Cox
Kate Jackson

ROCKY — Leonardo DiCaprio
Richard Paul

ROGAN — Dirk Bogarde

ROKER — Arthur Taxier

ROLLO — Jack London
Teddy Roosevelt

ROOSEVELT — Sally Kellerman

ROSALITA — Kevin Costner

Kevin Costner's Labrador retriever Rosalita is the daughter of Rocky, the dog who played Kevin's dog in the film *Revenge*.

ROSIE — Brenda Vaccaro

ROVER — Dorothy Gish
Lyndon Johnson
George Washington

George Washington's favorite dog, whose fame became so great that his name became synonymous with "dog." Rover was "first to sleep, first to bark and first in the hearts of his countrymen."

ROXANNE — Michael Landon

ROXIE — Morgan Brittany

ROXY — Eydie Gorme
Steve Lawrence

ROYAL — Sir Walter Scott

RUBY — Bea Arthur
Stephen Crane
Martina Navratilova
Anais Nin

RUBY ROUGH — Calvin Coolidge

RUDY — Doris Day

RUFF — Dennis the Menace

RUFFY — Irene Dunne

RUFUS — Winston Churchill
Haunani Minn
Marc Singer

RUMPLES — Kathryn Grayson

RUMP ROAST — Melvin Belli

RUNGE — Maurice Sendak

RUSSIA — Bo Derek

RUSTY — David Hasselhoff
Mark Lindsay

RYAN — Mark Harmon
Greg Louganis

SACHA — Joe Conley
Ruth Gordon

SADIE — Barbra Streisand

After Barbra Streisand finished filming *Funny Girl*, the whole cast and crew pitched in to buy her Sadie, a toy poodle named after one of the songs in the movie, *Sadie, Sadie, Married Lady*.

SAILOR BOY
> Teddy Roosevelt

SAKKI   Amanda Bearse

SALE GOSSE
> Barbara Walters

SALLY   Richard Burton
> A. J. Cronin
> Elizabeth Taylor

SAM   Earl Holliman
> Patricia McPherson
> Minnie Pearl

SAMANTHA Cynthia Allison
> Joanne Carson
> Johnny Carson
> Mary McDonough
> Katharine Ross

SAMI   Patricia McCormack

SAMMY   Ken Maynard
> Tori Spelling

SAMSON   Laurie Burton
> William Devane
> James Thurber

SANDRINGHAM GLEN
> King George VI

SANDRINGHAM SCION
> King George VI

SANDRINGHAM SPARK
> King George V

SANDRINGHAM STOW
> King George V

SANDRINGHAM STREAM
> King George VI

SANDY Little Orphan Annie
> A. J. Cronin
> Gracie Fields

Gracie Fields moved to Italy, and because her dog Sandy disliked Italians, he made an excellent guard dog.

> Alice Roosevelt Longworth
> Beatrix Potter
> Patrick Wayne
> Woodrow Wilson

SANFORD III   Edie Adams

SARAH   Alfred Hitchcock

Alfred Hitchcock, legendary for such films as *The Birds*, had a West Highland terrier named Sarah, who was perhaps the only animal in Hollywood that refused to take direction from him.

> Vita Sackville-West

SARGEANT   Earl Holliman

SASCHA   Sid Caesar

SASHA   George Cukor
> Jennie Garth
> Ruta Lee
> Valerie Perrine

SATAN   Tennessee Williams

SAUDI   Brad Pitt

SAUKI   Zachary Ty Bryan

SAUVIGNON   Heloise

SCARLET   Staci Keanan
SCARLETT
                Richard Simmons
SCHATZIE   Bette Davis
                Doris Day
SCHELSCA   Dudley Moore
SCHLUBBER   Marlon Brando
SCHNICK   Vincent Price
SCHOTTZIE   Marge Schott

Schottzie, the Saint Bernard of Cincinnati Reds owner Marge Schott, is also the unofficial mascot of the team and gets tons of her own fan mail. Schottzie thinks nothing of putting on her own baseball cap, and taking the elevator down to the playing field on her own.

SCHUNYA   Bela Lugosi
SCOOTER
                Mary Kate McGeehan
SCOTCH   Ronald Reagan
                Jane Wyman
SCOTT   Tom Hayden
                Mark Lindsay
SCRUFFY   George DiCenzo
                Kathryn Grayson
                Leonard Maltin
                Mrs. Carolyn Muir
SCRUMMY   King George VI
SEARCHER
                George Washington

SEBASTIAN   Vivien Leigh
                Danny Radojevic
SHADOW   Corey Feldman
                Earl Holliman
SHAGGY   Harvey Korman
SHAKA   Blair Underwood
SHANDYGAFF   Jean Muir

Jean Muir's Scottish terrier Shandygaff's favorite drink was beer and ginger ale.

SHANE   Oprah Winfrey
SHANNON
                John F. Kennedy, Jr.
                Pia Zadora
SHARKEY   Shane Conrad
SHARP   Queen Victoria
SHEBA   Nelson Eddy
SHEEBA   Heloise
SHELBY   Bill Blass
SHELLEY   Aaron Spelling

Aaron Spelling is so crazy about his animals that one Christmas he purchased his daughter Tori, who also stars in his series *Beverly Hills 90210*, four little china Battersea boxes that he had specially made for her in England, each of which contained the portrait of a Spelling dog.

SHINKA   Meredith MacRae
                Greg Mullavey
SHIRA   Byron Scott

SHIRLEY	Kaye Ballard
	Michael Landon
SHOCK	John Gay
SHUTTZ	Willie Aames
SID	Max Gail
SIDNEY	Clint Eastwood
SILKY	David Hasselhoff
SILLY	Bobby Sherman
SILLY SALLY	
	Shannen Doherty
SIMBA	Jimmy Stewart
	Betty White
SIMON	Partridge Family
	Paul Muni

Paul Muni's airedale Simon knew the words "I'm going for a walk," and he would always run for the door. Thinking to outsmart him, Muni said it in Yiddish, but Simon still ran for the door! Paul never did learn where he picked up the second language.

	Billy Squier
SINHUE	Dirk Bogarde
SIRIUS	Denys Finch Hatton
SIR WINSTON	
	T. Boone Pickens
SISSY	David Hasselhoff
SKEEPER	David Holt
SKEETS	Brenda Vaccaro
SKILAKI	Marina Sirtis

Marina Sirtis, who played Deanna Troy on *Star Trek: TNG*, is half Greek, and that's why she named her tiny little Yorkie Skilaki, which means "little dog" in Greek.

SKIP	Teddy Roosevelt
SKIPPER	James Mason
SKIPPY	Elly May Clampett
SKOOKUN	Paul Bunyan
SKOSHIE	Marty Ingels
	Shirley Jones
SKY	Roger Staubach

Roger Staubach named his beagle Sky after Sky Ranch, the Dallas Cowboys headquarters where the dog was found. The dog likes jokes, and Roger always insists that anyone who meets him and Sky has to tell the dog a joke.

SLIPPER	Wallis Simpson
SLUGGY	Humphrey Bogart
SMILIN' SAM	David Cassidy

David Cassidy's favorite dog, called Sam for short, became the father of five puppies. With the help of *Tiger Beat* magazine, he found homes for all of the puppies with his fans.

SMOKE	Bo Derek
	Earl Holliman
SMOKEY	Paul Newman

SNIP	King George V
SNITTLE TIMBERY	
	Charles Dickens
SNOOPY	Charlie Brown
	Fred Keating
	Mary McDonough
	Elvis Presley
	Lisa Marie Presley
SNOW	Susan Strasberg
SNOWFLAKE	
	Gladys, Duchess
	of Marlborough
SNOW JOB	Bob Hope
SNOW WHITE	
	Janet Jackson
SNOWY	Doris Day
SNUFFY	Liberace
	Kelly Emberg
SNUGGER	Bo Derek
SOCRATES	
	Lady Ottoline Morrell
SODA	Ronald Reagan
	Jane Wyman
SOJAH	Tisha Campbell
SOLO	George Cukor
SONNIE	Herbert Hoover
SONNY	Eydie Gorme
	Steve Lawrence
SOONER	Betty White
SOPHIE	James Thurber
SOUCI	Colette
SOUFFLE	Ethel Kennedy

SPANKY	Bruce Penhall
SPANNEL	The Mayflower

When the Mayflower arrived in America in 1620, one of the first to land on Plymouth Rock was Spannel, a staunchly Puritan dog who was fleeing from religious persecution in England.

SPARKEY	Rhonda Fleming
SPARKLE	Kirk Douglas
	Gilda Radner
	Gene Wilder
SPARKY	Sheena Easton
SPENCER	
	Kareem Abdul-Jabbar
SPICE	Della Reese
SPIKE	Joan Rivers

Nothing is too good for Joan Rivers Yorkie Spike, who eats off Limoges china and rides in a Louis Vuitton carrier.

SPOOKY	Mel Torme
SPORT	Anais Nin
	Kate Smith
SPOT	Linda Darnell
	Dick & Jane
	Carol Lawrence
	Rob Lowe
	Beatrix Potter
	Elizabeth Taylor
	Queen Victoria
SPUDS MACKENZIE	
	Budweiser

SPUNKY
Dwight D. Eisenhower

SPUTNIK   Charles James

STAN   David Letterman

Even though late night talk show comedian David Letterman is famous for, among other things his "Stupid Pet Tricks" segments, his own dog Stan has never appeared in one.

STANLEY   Alfred Hitchcock

STAR   Wayne Rogers
        Sylvia Sidney

STASI   Adolf Hitler

STERLING   William Shatner

STEVIE WONDERFUL
    Charlotte Mailliard Swig

STICKEEN   John Muir

STIFFY   King George VI

STORMY   Betty White

STRANGE   Patrick McManus

STREAKER   John F. Kennedy

STREUDEL
    Arnold Schwarzenegger

STRICTE   Actaeon

The hounds of Actaeon are an integral part of Greek mythology. One of the dogs is Stricte, whose name translates from Greek to English as "Spot!"

STRUDEL   James Dean

SUE   Queen Elizabeth II

SUGAR   Ann-Margret
        Queen Elizabeth II
        Della Reese
        Elizabeth Taylor

SULTAN   Charles Dickens

SUMMA   Pat Boone

SUMNER   Axl Rose

SUNNEE   Walt Disney

SUNNYBANK
    Albert Payson Terhune

SUNNYBANK JEAN
    Albert Payson Terhune

SUNNYBANK SIGURD
    Albert Payson Terhune

SUNSHINE   Susan Strasberg
        David L. Wolper

SUSHIE   Barbra Streisand

SUSIE   Zsa Zsa Gabor
        Bobby Sherman

SUZETTE   Liberace

SUZIE   Gracie Allen
        George Burns
        Cary Grant

Cary Grant was whisked away by Howard Hughes in his private airplane, of which Howard was also the pilot, so that Cary could marry Betsy Drake. She had no one to stand up for her, so she was given away by her wedding gift from Cary—a white poodle named Suzie.

	Al Pacino
SUZIE WONG	Liberace
SUZY	Jack Wagner
SWALLOW	
	William Wordsworth
SWEETHEART	King Lear
SWEETIE	Carrie Fisher
SWEETLIPS	
	George Washington
T-BONE	Lucius Beebe
TABBY	Tad Lincoln
TACA	Ronald Reagan
TAFFERTEFY	
	King George VI
TALBOT	King Arthur
TANDY	Harry S. Truman
TARA	Rex Harrison
	Charlton Heston
	Jack Scalia
TARZAN	
	Edgar Rice Burroughs
TASHA	Barbara Mandrell
TASTER	George Washington
TATTERS	Earl Holliman
TAXI	Tom Hayden
TEDDY	Ingmar Bergman
	Charlie Chaplin
	Kirk Douglas
	Nell Shipman
TELEK	
	Dwight D. Eisenhower

TERESA	Julie Harris
TESS	Lily Tomlin
TESSA	James Thurber
THANE	
	Albert Payson Terhune
THE MOOTER	Jackie Joseph
THENNE	Brigitte Bardot
THERON	Actaeon
THOMAS A. BECKET	
	Richard Burton
	Elizabeth Taylor
TIAPKA	Ivana Trump
TIAPKA II	Ivana Trump

Ivana Trump's doggie Tiapka, which means "paw" in her native Czechoslovakian, knows how to make sure he is not left behind. He knows that a certain gray suitcase always goes on trips, so he just gets into the bag, and off he goes!

TIDA	Phil Donahue
TIFFANY	Diana Ross
	Aaron Spelling
TIGE	Buster Brown
TIGER	David Cassidy
	Doris Day
	Judith Campbell Exner
	Marc Jacobs

Clothing designer Marc Jacobs used his pooch Tiger as the inspiration for a line of dalmatian print sweaters which he designed for Perry Ellis.

Catherine the Great, Empress of all Russia, was so devoted to her dog Tom Anderson that when he died she had an Egyptian pyramid erected to house his remains.

TIGGER	Prince Charles
	Emily McLaughlin
TILLIE	Matthew Margolis
TIM	Mikhail Baryshnikov
TIMBER DOODLE	
	Charles Dickens
TIMMY	Princess Grace
TIMOTHY	Dorothy Parker
	Betty White
TINA	Darryl Zanuck
TINKERBELL	Lucille Ball
TINKER TOY	Lucille Ball
TINY	Doris Day
	Franklin Delano Roosevelt
TINY TIM	Calvin Coolidge
TIP	Mia Farrow
TIPLER	George Washington
TIPPIE	Elaine Princi
TIPPY	Marilyn Monroe
TITO	Bela Lugosi
TOBY	King Arthur
	Burgess Meredith
	John Steinbeck
TOBY-CHIEN	Colette
TODD POTTER	Brad Pitt
TOKI	Pia Zadora
TOLSTOY	Susan Butcher
TOM ANDERSON	
	Catherine the Great

TONKA	Meredith MacRae
	Greg Mullavey
TONY	Marj Dusay
	George Gershwin
	Charlton Heston
	June Lockhart
	Mary Pickford
TOOTI	Meredith MacRae
	Greg Mullavey
TOPPER	Tom Selleck
TORO	Charo
TOTO	Dorothy Gale
	David Hasselhoff
	Paul Muni
TOUGH	Bo Derek
TOWSER	Kent Fowler
TOY	Lucille Ball
	Maria Callas
TRACIE	Robert Herrick
TRAY	King Lear
TREACLE	Agatha Christie
TREVOR	William Howard Taft
TRILLION	Harris Katleman
TRIP	Harriet Beecher Stowe
TRIXIE	Doris Day

TROUBLE
F. Scott Fitzgerald
Zelda Fitzgerald

TROWNEER   King Arthur

TRUELOVE
George Washington

TRUMP   William Hogarth

TSAR   Christopher Lee

TUCK   James Dean

TULIP   J. R. Ackerley

TUMBER   Charles Dickens

TUPPINSKY   Shelley Duvall

TURI   Queen Victoria

TURK   Charles Dickens

TWINKY   Corey Feldman

TYLER   Henry Kissinger

Henry Kissinger's dog was often blamed for his master being perpetually late to meetings, but Henry defended Tyler, stating that the dog actually got up first. Tyler was also known for gobbling down the Secret Service men's sandwiches.

TZUTSEE   Beatrix Potter

UBU   Gary David Goldberg

Gary David Goldberg, the creator of the TV series *Family Ties*, named his "Ubu Productions" company after his pet pooch. At the end of every episode, viewers would hear the phrase "Sit, Ubu, sit" while the company logo was run.

ULLI   Matthew Margolis

VALENTINE Roger Horchow

VARMIT   Doris Day

VENUS   Chuck Eisenmann

VERA   Stan Lee

VETO   James A. Garfield

Garfield's dog Veto was a rather discriminating listener, and when he disapproved of Charles Dickens' rendition of his poem *A Christmas Carol*, he began barking. The President thought this was so hysterical that for months afterward, whenever he saw someone who was at the event, he would start barking like a dog.

VICKY   Richard Nixon
Vincent Price

VICTORY   Ronald Reagan

VIGI   King Olaf

VIRGIL THOMSON
John Houseman

VIVIEN LEIGH Jaclyn Smith

VLAD THE IMPALER   Elvira

VULCAN
George Washington

WALLY   Staci Keanan
Bobby Sherman

WANG	Happy Rockefeller
WAT	Princess Beatrice
WAWE	Merle Haggard
WEEJIE	Herbert Hoover
WEINER	David Hasselhoff
WELDEMANN	
	Queen Victoria
WENDEL	Brian Keith
WESSEX	Thomas Hardy
WHIP	Barry Diller
WHISKERS	Tom Weiskopf
WHISKEY	George Brent
	Don Galloway
Senator Daniel P. Moynihan	
	Ann Todd
WHITE ANGEL	
	Peggy Guggenheim
WHITE CHRISTMAS	
	P. Pruett
WHITE FANG	Soupy Sales
WHITE KING	Thelma Todd
WHITE TIPS	
	Caroline Kennedy
WHOOPEE	Lucille Ball
WICKLE	Lucie Arnaz
WILD WILLIE	Axl Rose
WILLIAM	Rex Harrison
	Lilli Palmer
WILLIE	Allen Ludden
	Betty White

WINDSOR BOB
King George VI

WINKIE   Claudette Colbert

WINKS
Franklin Delano Roosevelt

WINNIE   Edmund Lowe

WINSTON   Jimmy Barker

WOLF   Sigmund Freud
John F. Kennedy
Dorothy Parker
Albert Payson Terhune

Author Albert Payson Terhune wrote extensively about canine heroes, and in real life his collie Wolf was also a hero. Wolf saved the life of an intinerant dog who was about to be hit by a train, losing his own life in the process.

Rip Van Winkle

WOLFIE
Representative Pat Schroeder

WOLVERTON BEN
King George V

WOLVERTON JET
King George V

WOODROW WILSON
Dorothy Parker

WOODY   Robin Riker

WOTAN   Charlton Heston

WRINKLES   Liberace
Michael Landon

XENOPHON
     Couve De Murville

XERXES   Queen Alexandra

YANG   Ringo Starr

YANKEE DOODLE
     Ginger Rogers

YING   Ringo Starr

YONEX Martina Navratilova

YOU KNOW   Mark Twain

YOUKI   Brigitte Bardot

YUKI   Lyndon Johnson

Lyndon Johnson slept with Yuki, one of the few Presidents who would sleep with his dog. He never left the White House without at least one pooch, and they rode with him in his limousines, helicopters and airplanes. Johnson insisted his dogs attend all White House functions, and they were fed off their own silver trays.

YUKON   Herbert Hoover

YUKON KING
  Sergeant William Preston

YUNKO   Bela Lugosi

ZACK   Jennie Garth
    Barbara Walters

ZANDRA Barbara Lazaroff
    Wolfgang Puck

ZAR   Steffi Graf

ZARGON
    Olivia Newton-John

ZEACH George Washington

ZELDA   Mark Lindsay

ZERO   Little Annie Rooney
    Barry Gibb

ZEUS   Mrs. Debbie Fields
    Robbin Masters

ZINFANDEL   Heloise

The Heloise from the internationally syndicated *Hints from Heloise* created a sensation when her schnauzer went on a diet. His "before" and "after" diet photos ultimately appeared in Good Housekeeping magazine, leading to Zinfandel's developing not only a small waistline but also a huge following of his own.

ZIP   Paul Bunyan

ZOE   Shelley Duvall

ZONA   Gladys, Duchess
    of Marlborough

ZORA   Gary Cooper

ZORRO Douglas Fairbanks
    Mary Pickford

ZOZO Betsy Bloomingdale

Socialite Betsy Bloomingdale is very concerned about the diet of her German Shepherd Zozo, so the dog eats special meals that a canine nutritionist brings to the house.

ZSA ZSA GABOR
                   Ricki Lake

ZURCHA Vita Sackville-West

ZUZU   Martha Stewart

CAT

NAMES

ADMETUS	T. S. Eliot
AGRIPPINA	Agnes Repplier
AJAX	Nanette Fabray
ALADDIN	Gladys Taber
ALBERT THE GOOD	
	Vincent Price
ALICE	Earl Holliman

Earl Holliman is the power behind "Actors and Others for Animals." One of their major programs is to ensure that pets are neutered. According to Earl, if you let a cat have kittens and the kittens have kittens, in seven years you will have 36,000 cats from that one kitten.

John Lennon

The fate of John Lennon's cat should be a warning to all apartment dwellers. When he and Yoko Ono lived at the Dakota, Alice fell out of their window, and they lived too many stories up for even this cat's nine lives.

Yoko Ono

ALLEY CAT	
	Ernest Hemingway
ALLISON	Frankie Valli
AMBER	George Booth
	Merle Oberon
	Gladys Taber

AMY	Edward Gorey
ANGEL	Franco Columbu
	Victoria Jackson

Victoria Jackson became very depressed when she didn't get the part at an audition, so she immediately went across the street to an animal shelter and adopted Angel to cheer her up.

ANGUS SILKY	James Mason
	Pamela Mason
ANNA	James Mason
	Pamela Mason
ANNIE	Jeff Conaway
	Ricki Lake
ANTHONY	
	Robert Delaunay
APPOLLINARIS	Mark Twain
ARCHIBALD BUCHANAN	
	Pamela Mason
ARIEL	Andrew Lang
ARTHUR	Jeane Kirkpatrick
ASHLEY	Tara Buckman
	Regis Philbin
	Vanna White
ASOLE	Joan Van Ark
ASPARAGUS	T. S. Eliot
ATHENAEUM	
	John Middleton Murray
ATOSSA	Matthew Arnold
AUGUSTA	Mary E. Wilkins

AVERY   Mills Watson

AXL   Jason James Richter

BAAL   Jim Belushi

BABA   Sally Struthers

BABOU   Colette

BABY   James Mason

BABY MEW   Jackie Joseph

BALI   Erik Estrada

BANJO   Ella Wheeler Wilcox

BARNABY   Jerry Herman

BARRE-DE-ROUILLE
          Joris-Karl Huysmans

BATHSHEBA
     John Greenleaf Whittier

John Greenleaf Whittier wrote the epitaph for Bathsheba: "To whom none ever said scat, No worthier cat, Ever sat on a mat; Or caught a rat; Requies-cat."

BEAR   Lisa Hartman

Lisa Hartman's cat Bear likes to slide across the floor the way a baseball player slides into home plate.

BEBOP   Valeria Golino

BEDFORD   Tammy Grimes
                Rex Harrison

BEE BEE   Tanya Roberts

Tanya Roberts is such a cat lover that she would never marry anyone who didn't like cats.

BEEBE   Earle Larimore

BEELZEBUB   Mark Twain

In naming his cat Beelzebub, Mark Twain was not paying homage to the devil, but simply wanted to teach his children how to pronounce this difficult word from the Bible.

BELAUD Joachim Du Bellay

BELLA   Patrick Stewart

BES MUDI   Errol Flynn

BETSY   Yeardley Smith

BETTI   Joel Grey

BIANCA   Julia Campbell
                Frankie Valli

BIJOU   Colette

BILBO   Mariette Hartley

BILL   Robert Mandan

BILLY   Willie Aames
                Edward Gorey

BING CLAWSBY
          Michael Feinstein

BISCUIT   Joel Bailey
                Gina Gallego

BISMARK
      Florence Nightingale

BLACK & WHITE
          Devon Gummersall

BLACK BEAU
Lee Meriwether

Lee Meriwether's cat Black Beau had 14 toes on its front paws, seven on each side. Her daughter used to charge the other children in the neighborhood to see the toes on the cat.

BLACK CAT   Doris Lessing

BLACKIE   Winston Churchill
Calvin Coolidge
Lou Costello

BLACK KITTY
Richard Basehart

BLACKY   Matthew Arnold

BLATHERSKITE   Mark Twain

BLAZE   Calvin Coolidge

BLONDIE   Tanya Roberts
Red Skelton

BLUE EYES
Mrs. Debbie Fields

BLUEGRASS   Daniel Boone

BOB   Bob Hope

BOCHE   Anne Frank

BOISE   Ernest Hemingway

Ernest Hemingway's cat Boise, addicted to various drugs, constantly pestered Hemingway for vitamin B capsules and blood-pressure tablets, and couldn't go to sleep without Seconal.

BONA MARIETTA
Robert Southey

BONITA   Yeardley Smith

BOO BOO   Daryl Anderson

BOO-BOO KITTY
Shirley Feeney

BOO-DYES
Mrs. Debbie Fields

BOOTS   Carol Lawrence

BOOTSY   Le Var Burton

BORAX   Nanette Fabray

BORIS   Robin Eisenman

BOSCO   George Gobel

BOUNDER   Calvin Coolidge

BRANDO   Bonnie Bedelia

BRIE   Bill Meyers

BRILLO   Nanette Fabray

BRUCE   Fannie Flagg

BRUNO   Wes Craven

BUBBER   Ann-Margret

BUBIE   Robin Eisenman

BUCKWHEAT
Patricia McPherson

BUCKY   Tanya Roberts

BUFFALO BILL   Mark Twain

BUFFY   Ray Bradbury

BUNS   Victoria Principal
Tanya Roberts

BUSTER   Fred Bergendorff

BUSTOPHER JONES
                    T. S. Eliot

BUTCH   Joel Hirschorn

CABOODLE
        Marianne Gordon
              Kenny Rogers

Pet love knows no greater bounds than Kenny Rogers, who, even though he is allergic to cats, still has two furry friends. It takes a lot of shots and keeping the windows open for Kenny to "live" with all of his pets.

CACTUS JACK Ray Bradbury

CADILLAC   Isiah Thomas

CALICO   Joan Fontaine

CALVIN
        Charles Dudley Warner

CALVIN PEOPLES
             Gabrielle Carteris

CAMEMBERT   Bill Beyers

CARRREAM   Joan Van Ark

CARUSO   Roberta Flack

CAT BALLOU   Peggy McKay

CATARINA   Edgar Allan Poe

CATO   Lindsay Wagner

CELESTINE
              Rue McClanahan

Rue McClanahan noticed a man throwing a cat into an alley. She asked him if he was throwing it away, and when he said yes, she grabbed Celestine and ran for it.

CHAMPAGNE
              Bobbie Bresee

CHAN   Gerald Ford

CHANG   Cindy Williams

CHANG MAI
          Sally Jessy Raphael

CHANOINE   Victor Hugo

CHARLES O'MALLEY
            Michael Joseph

CHARLIE   Ava Cadell
              Edward Gorey
              Pamela Mason
              Shelley Smith

CHARLIE BROWN
                 Liz Taylor

CHARLIE CHAPLIN
              Estelle Taylor

CHARO   Yoko Ono

CHEESELER   Jay Leno

For Christmas one year, Jay Leno got his cat Cheeseler a special cat video. Cheeseler was reportedly so infatuated with the tape, he took control of the remote control, got a beer, sat in Jay's chair, and wouldn't let Jay watch his own show on TV.

CHEETAH   Earl Holliman

CHILLA   Paul Gallico

CHILLY WILLY
David Lascher

CHIN Paul Gallico

CHO CHO
Billy Dee Williams

CHOCOLATE CHIP
Jay Osmond

CHOICE Janis Ward

CHOPIN F. Scott Fitzgerald
Zelda Fitzgerald

CHRISSY Suzanne Somers

CHRISTOPHER Frankie Valli

Frankie Valli's cat Christopher likes to walk back and forth on the keys of his piano. Unfortunately, Frankie has never been able to use any of the cat's tunes in his act.

CICCIO Bill Conti

CINEMA Peggy McKay

CLARENCE Stephen Dorff
Frances Farmer

CLARK Tracy Bregman

CLEMENTINE
Yeardley Smith

CLEO Richard Burton
Meredith MacRae
Greg Mullavey
Elizabeth Taylor

Elizabeth Taylor's husband John Warner was very insistent that they move into the Watergate Hotel, which had a strict "no pets" policy. Liz decided that she'd rather have her little friends, and promptly filed for divorce.

CLEOPATRA
Lawrence Sanders

CLOTH CAP Pamela Mason

CLOTHILD THE USER
Roger A. Caras

COCO Ed Asner

Ed Asner uses his newspaper to launch pre-emptive strikes on other cats in the neighborhood, to protect his cats from being attacked.

COLLEEN Michael J. Fox

COLLETTE Yeardley Smith

COLUMBINE
Thomas Carlyle

COON DOG Bo Derek

CROCUS Brigitte Bardot

CRUMPET Meredith MacRae
Greg Mullavey

CUBA Ernest Hemingway

CUDDLES Kinky Friedman

CURTIS Amanda Bearse
Gloria DeHaven

CUTHBERT P. D. James

DAISY Gloria DeHaven
Gretchen Wyler

DAKI Gene Moore

DANCER	Walter Cronkite
DAPHNE	Lee Meriwether
DAVID	Gertrude Lawrence
DEMETER	T. S. Eliot
DICK	Amanda Bearse

Amanda Bearse, when she isn't starring in and directing the hit TV series *Married . . . With Children*, is an active force behind PAWS/LA, an organization that helps people with HIV to take care of their pets.

Frances Hodgson Burnett
DICKENS David Copperfield

David Copperfield would like to do a cat food commercial in which a cat magician makes a can of cat food appear right before your eyes.

DIGGER	Robin Riker
DINGO	Ray Bradbury
DISRAELI	Florence Nightingale
DITZIE	Ray Bradbury
DOLLY	Tallulah Bankhead
DOTTIE	Philece Sampler
DR. CARLTON B. FORBES	Steve Martin

Steve Martin's tiger-striped cat allegedly amassed $3,000 worth of cat toys by stealing checks from his mailbox. Unfortunately, he fled to Catalina via catamaran before Martin could bring him to justice.

DR. SCAT	Kinky Friedman
DREAMER	Willie Aames
DUDLEY	Ali MacGraw
DUKEY	David Groh
DWEEZIL	Robert Wagner

Personalities Moon Unit and Dweezil, offspring of rocker Frank Zappa, presented two cats, named after themselves, to movie star Robert Wagner and his cable VJ daughter Katie.

EARTHA CAT	Roger A. Caras
EASHIPUR	Dr. Boris Bagdassarroff
EL C.	Joan Van Ark
ELECTRA	T. S. Eliot
ELVIS	Kirstie Alley John Lennon
ENJOLRAS	Theophile Gautier
ENRIQUE DELOME	William McKinley
ESME	Gladys Taber
FACE	Pamela Mason
FAGIN	Jean Arthur
FATRICK	Gwen Verdon

FEATHERS Carl Van Vechten

FEETS FOSSE
Gwen Verdon

FELIMARE
Cardinal Richelieu

FERD   Robin Eisenman

FIDDLE   Joseph Kesselring

FIDDLER   Jacqueline Bisset

FIGARO   Loni Anderson

FIGAROE   Xavier Roberts

FILA   Jourdan Fremin

FISHER   Aleksandr Borodin

The Russian composer Aleksandr Borodin named his cat Fisher because of the feline's ability to grab fish out of the river.

FLASH   Patricia McPherson

FLAVIA   Sir Richard Steele

FLORA   Tallulah Bankhead

FLORENCE   Robert Mandan
James Taylor

FLUFF   David Groh

FLUFFY   John Ritter

FOEDRICKS   Marion Ross

FOLLY   James Mason

FOOGIE
Thomas Ian Nicholas

FOSHAY   Tomie De Paola

FOSS   Edward Lear

FRANK   Amanda Bearse
Katie Couric

FRED   Candice Bergen

FREDDIE   Red Skelton

FRIMBO   Charles Addams

FRITZ   Charles Osgood

FURBALL   Candice Bergen

FUSTO Adrienne Barbeau

GAINSBOROUGH
Edith Head

GAMMA   James Mason

GATO   Bob Barker

GAVROCHE
Theophile Gautier

GAZZA   Ray Bradbury

GENERAL FELIX
Mickey Rooney

GENT   Linda Evans

GENTLEMAN CALLER
Tennessee Williams

GEOFFREY
John D. MacDonald

GEORGE   Valerie Bertinelli
Edward Gorey
Cybill Shepherd
Eddie Van Halen
Andrew Lloyd Webber

GEORGE PUSHDRAGON
T. S. Eliot

GERONIMO   Barry Mann
Cynthia Weil

GILLY   Morgan Fairchild

GIN   Richard Lockridge

GINA   Bo Derek

GINGER   Jane Powell

Jane Powell's cat Ginger was extremely pleased when she and her master made the cover of *Life* magazine on September 6, 1946.

                Natalie Wood

GIORGIO
          Peggy Guggenheim

GIZMO   Shannon Miller

GLADSTONE

          Florence Nightingale

GODZILLA   Shirley Temple

GOERGE   Edward Gorey

GOOFY   Christopher Norris

GOO GOO   Dom DeLuise

GOUDA   Bill Beyers

GRACE   Christopher Walken

GRANDVIEW   Rick Schroder

GRAY PEARL   Ray Bradbury

GREAT RUMPUSCAT
                  T. S. Eliot

GRETA   Shelley Smith

GRIMALKIN   Benjamin West

GRIS-GRIS
          Charles De Gaulle

GRIZABELLA   T. S. Eliot

GROUCHO   Robert Donner

GROWLTIGER   T. S. Eliot

GUCCI   Erik Estrada

GUMBIE   T. S. Eliot

GUNTRY   Patricia Arquette

GUS   T. S. Eliot

GYP   Andrew Lang

GYPSY   Dick Clark
           Peggy Guggenheim
           Olivia Newton-John
                 Markie Post
                 Michael Ross

HAILEY   Love Hewitt

HAMILCAR   Anatole France

HAMLET   Thaao Penghlis

HARMONY   Carol Connors

HAROLD   Gretchen Wyler

HASKELL   Paula Poundstone

HECATE   Elvira

Cassandra Peterson, better known as Elvira, Mistress of the Dark, has named all of her companion animals in keeping with her stage persona. Hecate is named after the lead witch in *Macbeth*. Her other little friends are in the Dracula theme, starting with Vlad, Count Dracula himself, followed by Bela, after Bela Lugosi, the most famous screen Dracula, Bram, after Bram Stoker, the author of "Dracula" and Renfeld after the Count's bug-eating henchman.

HECTOR   Ray Bradbury

Ray Bradbury's cat Hector was very attached to his daughter. After she left home, Hector waited in the driveway for an entire year for her to return, jumping up every time he saw a Volvo, which was the make of Bradbury's daughter's car.

HERSHEY BAR
      Ed McMahon

HILLARY   Wes Craven

HINSE OF HINSEFIELD
      Sir Walter Scott

HOBO   Meredith MacRae
      Greg Mullavey

HODGE
      Dr. Samuel Johnson

HOLLY-GO-LIGHTLY
      Frances Farmer

Frances Farmer, the movie star of the 1930's, was subject to fits of depression which she tried to solve with alcohol. When a friend gave her a badly burned kitten, however, the kitten quickly won her over with its feeble attempts to move. Soon, she was consumed with getting up every three hours to administer its medicine, and she quit drinking in the process.

HOMER   Ken Burns

HONEY   Earl Holliman
      Bobby Sherman

HORIZON   Larry Hankin

HUD   Robert Mandan

HURLYBURLYBUSS
      Robert Southey

ICARUS   Muhammad Ali

ISOLDE
      Catherine Oxenberg

JACK   Amanda Bearse

JADE   Bo Derek

JASPER   Orson Bean

JAWS   Natalie Wood

JEEPERS CREEPERS
      Elizabeth Taylor

JEFFREY   Christopher Smart

JELLICLE CAT   T. S. Eliot

JELLYLORUM   T. S. Eliot

JENNIE   Earl Holliman

JENNYANYDOTS   T. S. Eliot

JEREMIAH   Donna Mills

JESSIE   Laurie Burton

JIGGER   Willie Aames

JILL   Elizabeth Taylor

JIMMY   Rene Auberjonois

JINGLES   Brooke Shields

JOAN PAWFORD
        Sally Struthers

JOLEY   George Burns

JOLSON   Victoria Jackson

JOSEPHINE   Vincent Price

JUNIOR   Gene Shalit

KAANALOA
        Christina Applegate

KAPOK   Colette

KASHKA   Deidre Hall

KATIE   Andy Warhol

KATJIA   Rosemary Joyce

KATRINA Lisa Marie Presley

KAWABA
       Lesley Ann Warren

KIDDLEYWINKEMPOOPS
        Thomas Hardy

KIKI   Eileen Ford

KILLER   Janet Leigh

KISHA   Orson Bean

KISSA   Pia Lindstrom

KIT   Marianne Gordon
        Kenny Rogers

KITTENS   Roger Horchow

    Catalog mogul Roger Horchow utilizes his kitten named Kittens and his dog Valentine in publicity and catalog shots, and they have also been painted by Roger Winter. These portraits always accompany the Horchows when they change residences.

KITTY   Catherine Bach
     Michael J. Travanti
      Daniel J. Travanti

KITTY BOO Lee Meriwether

KITTY CARLISLE   Bill Harris

KITTY DEAREST
       Sally Struthers

KITTY KAT David Hasselhoff

KIZMET   Jean LeClerc

KLIBAN   James Gunn

KRO   Colette

LA CHATTE   Colette

LA DERNIERE CHATTE
        Colette

LA TOUTEN   Colette

LADY   George Burns
      Kinky Friedman

LADY ARABELLA
   John Spencer Churchill

LADY GRIDDLEBONE
        T. S. Eliot

LADY LEEDS   James Mason

LEE CHAN   Richard Hatch

LELONG Aleksandr Borodin

LEO   Loni Anderson
     Gloria DeHaven

LEONARDO   Pia Lindstrom

LILITH   Stephane Mallarme

LILLIAN   Damon Runyon

LILLY   Dr. Samuel Johnson
            Philece Sampler

LILY   George Booth

LIMPY   Paul Gallico

LISA DOUGLAS   Eva Gabor

Eva Gabor, like other celebrities, has named her cat after one of her more famous roles, that of Lisa Douglas on the hit sitcom *Green Acres*. She believes in treating her pets like children, not animals. She says, "Darling, if you are not going to treat pets like people, don't have pets."

LITTLE CLAY   Amanda Blake

LOLLIPOP   Stephen Macht

LORD NELSON
              Robert Southey

Poet Laureate Robert Southey's cat started out as just Lord Nelson, but as his expertise in ferretting out rats became more proficient, he was elevated for his services in this regard to Baron, Viscount and finally to an Earldom.

LOUIE   Loni Anderson

LOUIS   Deborah Goodrich
                Natalie Wood

LOUIS XIV   James Dean

LOUISE   Marion Ross

LUCI   Richard Crenna

LUCY   Quincy Jones
              Nastassja Kinski

LUKE   Liz Smith

LULU   Orson Bean

LULU II   Paul Gallico

LUMP   Nancy Walker

LUSTRE   Andre Malraux

MACAVITY   T. S. Eliot

MADAME BIANCHI
              Robert Southey

MADAME BUTTERFLY
                 Will Barnet

MADAME CATALINI
              Robert Southey

MADAME THEOPHILE
            Theophile Gautier

MAGDA   Eva Gabor

MAGGIE   Natalie Wood

MAGIC   Rod McKuen

MAI TAI   Art Linkletter

MALBROUK
          Lady Ottoline Morrell

MANMALOTTA
               Ray Bradbury

MARBLES   Jonathan Brandis

MARCUS   James Dean

MARGATE
            Winston Churchill

MARIDADI   Roger A. Caras

MARILYN Whitney Houston

Whitney Houston dedicated her platinum album *Whitney* to two of her cats, Marilyn and Miste.

MARK   Robert Wagner

MARMALADE
                          Anne Bancroft
                          Mel Brooks

MARMELADE Ray Bradbury

MARTINI Richard Lockridge

MASTER OF GRAY
                          Andrew Lang

MATAPON   Emile Achard

MAX   Calvin Klein
                          Michelle Phillips
                          Shelley Smith

MAXFIELD BLUE
                Chuck Hemingway

MAYBELL   Earl Holliman

MAZEL   Estelle Getty

MA-ZUL   James Taylor

MCDERMOT   Captain Kidd

MCGEE   Kathleen Turner

MEATBALL   Jane Pauley

MEHITABEL
                Mikhail Baryshnikov

MEI MEI   Robert Mondavi

MELANCHOLY
                          Michael Gray

MELBA   Ann-Margret

MENO   Harry Hamlin

MEPHISTOPHELES
                          Doris Lessing

MERLIN   Ali MacGraw

MICETTO   Chateaubriand
                          Pope Leo XII

MICHAEL   Roger A. Caras

MICK   Morgan Fairchild

MIKE THE MAGICAT
                          Harry S Truman

MILLIE   Marty Ingels
                          Shirley Jones

MILTIE   Pamela Mason

MIMI   Ed Reingold

MIMIE PAILLOU
                Cardinal Richelieu

MINA MINA JOSEPH
                          Michael Joseph

MINETTE   Gottfried Mind

MINI-MINI   Colette

MINIOONE   Colette

MINOUCHE   Emile Zola

MISHA   Yoko Ono

MISS ABIGAIL   Ed Asner

MISS CHIEF
                Susan Richardson

MISS HIT   Pamela Mason

MISS JENKINS
                Barbara Whinnery

MISS KITTY   Edith Fellows

MISS LUCY   Doris Day

MISS MAIS OUI
     Lauren Hutton

MISS PITTY   Julie Parrish

MISS PUSS PUSS Eva Gabor

MISS PUSSY
     Rutherford B. Hayes

MISTE   Whitney Houston

MISTEBLU
     Whitney Houston

MISTER   Earl Holliman

MISTER ROOTS
     Fannie Flagg

MISTER SHIPS   Liz Smith

MISTY GREY
     Mariel Hemingway

MISTY MALARKY YING
YANG   Amy Carter

MITLER   Marion Ross

MITSOU   Arthur Miller
     Marilyn Monroe

Sometimes it's a problem being famous. When her cat went into labor, Marilyn couldn't find a vet to deliver the babies. When she said on the phone, "This is Marilyn Monroe, my cat's having kittens," they all thought it was a crank call and hung up.

MITTONS   Billy Crystal

MO   James Gunn

MOLLY   Ava Cadell

MOMCAT   K Callan
     Michael Callan

MONROE   Earl Holliman
     Chris Lemmon

MONSTER   Brian McRae

MONSTRELLO
     Jacqueline Bisset

MONTY   Ed McMahon

MOON   Robert Wagner

MOORTJE   Anne Frank

MORGAN   Shelley Taylor

MORRIS   Mike Farrell
     Paul Gallico
     Ruta Lee

MOUCHE
     Joris-Karl Haysmans
     Victor Hugo

MOUMOUTTE BLANCHE
     Pierre Loti

MOUMOUTTE CHINOISE
     Pierre Loti

MOUSCHI   Anne Frank

MOUSE   James Taylor

MR. BLUE
     Roddy McDowall

MR. ESSEX   Ed Asner

MR. FEATHER PUSS
     Ernest Hemingway

MR. LUCKY   Doris Day

MR. MISTOFFOLEES
T. S. Eliot

MR. PEEPERS   Edith Fellows

MR. PETER WELLS
H. G. Wells

MR. TOBY   Andrew Lang

MRS. WIGGS   Edith Fellows

MUENSTER   Bill Beyers

MUEZZA   Mohammed

The prophet Mohammed's favorite cat Muezza was sleeping on his arm, and rather than disturb his sleep, Mohammed cut off his sleeve. When he returned, the cat thanked him, and Mohammed then touched his back three times, giving him three times three, or nine lives. This legend has come down to the present day.

MUFFIN   Kate Vernon

MUIDO   Pechuel Loesche

MUNGOJERRIE   T. S. Eliot

MUNKUSTRAP   T. S. Eliot

MUNSON   Joan Van Ark

MURR   E.T.A. Hoffmann

MUSCAT   Colette

MUSH   Pamela Mason

MYSOUFF
Alexandre Dumas

Alexandre Dumas, the author of *The Three Musketeers*, always maintained that his cat Mysouff was clairvoyant.

NATASHA   Robin Eisenman

NELLIE BLY   Kim Cattrall

NELSON   Winston Churchill

Winston Churchill was embarrassed by his dog Nelson. Even though he had given him the name of one of England's greatest heroes, during the London Blitz nothing could persuade the cowardly pooch to come out from under the bed.

NEMO
Prime Minister Harold Wilson

NERONE   W. H. Auden

NEW   Vivien Leigh
Laurence Olivier

NICHOLS   Vivien Leigh

NICKIE   James M. Cain

NICKY   Deborah Goodrich

NICOLE   Shirley Temple

NINJA   Mariah Carey

NOEL   Richard Basehart

NONAME   Noel Behn

NONOCHE   Colette

NOODLE   Robert Donner

NUTTY   Ray Bradbury

O-FER   Brian McRae

OEDIPUS BRUISER
                  Brendan Fraser

OLD DEUTERONOMY
                  T. S. Eliot

OLGA   Cybill Shepherd

OLIVER   Ray Bradbury
              Daniel J. Travanti

OLIVER JUNIOR
                  Barry Mann
                  Cynthia Weil

OOTS   Leslie Easterbrook

ORANGE CAT   Roger Ebert

ORANGE OLIVER
                  Linda Gray

OTHELLO   Robert Southey

OVID   Robert Southey

P2   K Callan

PANDORA   Clayton Moore

PANSY   P. D. James

PANTHER Rue McClanahan

PASCAL   Anatole France

PATCHES   Stephen Dorff
           Chuck Hemingway
           Marilyn Knowlden

PAWS   K Callan
            Michael Callan

PEACHES Barbara Mandrell

PEEK-ABOO
            Cora Sue Collins

PENQUIN   Bo Derek

PEPE   Robert Wagner

PEPPER   Betty Garrett

PEPPERPOT   Thomas Hood

PERCY   Karel Capek

PERRUQUE
            Cardinal Richelieu

PERSIAN   Marilyn Monroe

PERSIAN SNOW
            Erasmus Darwin

PETE   Richard Lockridge

PETEPEETOO
            Robert Indiana

PETEY   Pamela Mason

PETITEU   Colette

PETTIPAWS   T. S. Eliot

PHILIP   Karel Capek

PHILIPPE   Jean Arthur

PHOEBE   Earl Holliman

PICHINETTE   Colette

PICKLEPUSS
         Margaret Cooper Gay

PILAR   Ernest Hemingway

PING   Christopher Norris

PINKY   Ruta Lee

PIPPERS   George Booth

PISSED OFF   Bo Derek

PITIPOO   Paul Gallico

PITTI-SING
         Lilian Jackson Braun

PIXEL   Robert A. Heinlein

PLUTO   Edgar Allan Poe

POLAR BEAR
           Cleveland Amory

PONG   Christopher Norris

POO JONES   Vivien Leigh

POO-BAH
           Lilian Jackson Braun

POOH   Quinn Cummings

POPPET   Joe Namath

POWDERPUFF
           Tanya Roberts

PRECIOUS   Jeannie Wilson

PRET   Rev. J.G. Wood

PRETTY WHITE Orson Bean

PRINCE IGOR   Kate Vernon

PRINCESS
           Ernest Hemingway

PRINCESS SOPHIE LOUISE
     John Spencer Churchill

PRINCESS SQUADDLE
           Pamela Mason

PUDDY   Merv Griffin
             Juliet Prowse

PUDLENKA   Karel Capek

PUFF   Dick & Jane
             Pamela Mason

PUFFING   James Taylor

PUFFINS   Woodrow Wilson

PULCHERIA   Robert Southey

PURCY   Jackie Joseph

PURDOE   Samuel Butler

PUSSM   Jonathan Brandis

PUSSY GALORE
             Orson Bean

PUSSYCAT   Edward Anhalt

PUZZLE   Eddie Furlong

QUARTZ   Teddy Roosevelt

QUAXO   T. S. Eliot

QUEEN DI   Pamela Mason

QUEEN TUT   Ed McMahon

QUENTIN   Rick Schroder

QUINN   Barry Mann
               Cynthia Weil

RACAN   Cardinal Richelieu

RAGGEDY ANN
             Louise Nevelson

RAMAAHIPATI IV
             Greer Garson

RASCAL   Leigh Lawson

RATZO   Shelley Taylor

REBEL   Marty Ingels
              Shirley Jones

RENFELD DRACU   Elvira

RENFIELD   Jay Johnson

RENO   Barbara Bach

RHADAME   W. H. Auden

RHETT BUTLER
             Vanna White

RINGO   Dennis Weaver

ROADIE	Jennie Garth
ROCKY	Robert Davenport
	Barry Mann
	Wil Shriner
	Cynthia Weil
ROGER	John D. MacDonald
ROGUE	Karel Capek
ROMEO	
	Mary Frances Crosby
	Peggy Guggenheim

RUM TUM TUGGER
T. S. Eliot

RUMPELSTILZCHEN
Robert Southey

RUMPLES   Robert Southey

RUMPLETEAZER   T. S. Eliot

RUSTY   Bruce Boxleitner

Bruce Boxleitner is such a cat lover that he married a woman named Kitty.

	Elly May Clampett
	Ozzie Smith
RUTH	Pamela Mason
S.C.	Veronica Lake

Veronica Lake's cat's name S.C. stands for "Solid Citizen," and he gained some celebrity of his own. With six toes on each of his front paws, Ripley thought the cat of sufficient notoriety to put him into his *Believe It or Not.*

SABO	Stella Stevens
SADIE	Eva Gabor
	James Mason
	Dudley Moore
SAHA	Colette
SAKI	Paul Newman
	Joanne Woodward
SALEM	Kim Cattrall
SALOME	Tanya Roberts
SAM	Jean Arthur
	Adrienne Barbeau
SAMANTHA	
	Helen Gurley Brown
	Marty Ingels
	Shirley Jones
	Jonathan Taylor Thomas
SANS LENDEMAIN	
	Peggy Guggenheim
	James Joyce
SARA	Jamie Lyn Bauer
SAROYA	Barry Mann
	Cynthia Weil
SASCHA	Yoko Ono
	Regis Philbin
SASSY	Linda Evans
SAUSAGE	Patrick Stewart
SAVORTOOTH	
	George Booth
SCAMP	Karel Capek
SCAMPER	Brooke Adams
SCARLET	Regis Philbin

SCHEHERAZADE
Carl Van Vechten

SCHNITZ   Bruce Boxleitner

SCOTTY   Sally Struthers

SCRATCH   Kelly LeBrock

SCRATCHAWAY
Thomas Hood

SELIMA   Horace Walpole

SEÑOR   Stefanie Powers

SEYMOUR
Lawrence Sanders

SHAN   Gerald Ford

SHARKY   Dom DeLuise

SHAYNA   Estelle Getty

SHE   Bo Derek
Linda Evans

SHEBA   Sally Jessy Raphael

SHELLY   Sean Astin

SHERLOCK   Alexis Gershwin

SHERRY   Richard Lockridge

SHIVA   Chef Saad Chazi

SIAFU   Roger A. Caras

SIMBA   Gretchen Wyler

SIR JOHN LANGBOURNE
Jeremy Bentham

SIR JOHN RUMPALO
George Booth

SIZI   Albert Schweitzer

Albert Schweitzer was left-handed, but he had to learn to write with his right hand when his cat Sizi decided that his left arm was her favorite place to sleep.

SKEEZIX   Bree Walker

SKIMBLESHANKS   T. S. Eliot

SKIPPER   Jean Arthur

SKITTLES   Kristi Yamaguchi

SKUNK   Ernest Hemingway

SLEATOR   Kathleen Beller

SLIPPERS   Teddy Roosevelt

Teddy Roosevelt's cat Slippers was given the run of the White House, and he often chose to sleep right in the middle of the hall. On political occasions, visiting dignitaries—even foreign heads of state—were required to tiptoe around the slumbering kitty.

SMOKEY   Jack Cassidy
Shirley Jones
Rick Schroder

SMOKY   Koko the Gorilla
Ruta Lee

SMUDGE   John Gardner

SNEAKERS   Doris Day

SNOWDOVE
Thomas Hardy

SNUG HARBOR
Joan Van Ark

SOCKS
President Bill Clinton

SONGBIRD   Carol Connors

SONNY   Mary Jo Catlett

SOOTIKINS   Thomas Hood

SOPHIE   Robert Donner

SOPHOCLES   Ray Bradbury

SOUMISE
Cardinal Richelieu

SOUR MASH   Mark Twain

SPIC & SPAN
Nanette Fabray

SPIDER   James Mason

SPIKE   Rose Harris

SPITHEAD   Sir Isaac Newton

SPORTS FAN   Roger Ebert

SQUEAKY   Michael Brandon
Lee Purcell

STEVE   Mark Harmon

STINK   James Mason

STINKY   Morgan Fairchild

STRIPES   Lorraine Bracco

SUA   Robert Mandan

SUCKER   Stephen Macht

SUGAR   Jack Nicholson

SUKIE   Edward Gorey

SUMFUN ABIGAIL
Roger A. Caras

SUNNY   Jill St. John

SUPER CAT   Janet Gaynor

SUPERBOY   Eva Gabor

SUSHI   Jourdan Fremin
Henry Sanders

SUZANNE   Liz Smith

SUZIE   Stella Stevens

SWEDEN   K Callan

SWEET PEA   Al Kasha

SWEET WHITE   Orson Bean

SYBIL   Markie Post
Mr. Rogers

SYLVESTER   Melissa Gilbert

SYLVIA   Laurie Burton

T.K.   Betty White

T2   Eddie Furlong

TABITHA   Cynthia Harvey

TABITHA LONGCLAWS
Thomas Hood

TABITHA TWICHET
Pamela Mason

TABITHA TWITCHIT
Beatrix Potter

TAKI   Raymond Chandler

TALLULAH   Fannie Flagg

TALULLAH   Lorna Patterson

TAMA   Lafcadio Hearn

TAMMANY   Mark Twain

TANGO   Winston Churchill

TANTE HEDWIG
Paul Gallico

TARA	Jack Albertson
TATER	Ray Bradbury
TAYLOR	Tony Geary
TEDDY BEAR	Ed Asner
TEEGY	Tammy Grimes
TEENEY	Martha Stewart
TERRA CATTA	
	Victoria Principal
THE ONE AND ONLY	
	Colette
THE PEACH	Tammy Grimes
THOMAS	Bob Barker
THOMPKINS	Mariah Carey
THUNDER	
	Olivia Newton-John
TIDBITS	Gwen Verdon
TIFFANY	Dom DeLuise

Dom DeLuise's cat Tiffany, named after the fashionable store, will only eat the food of the family dog Midnight. When she isn't stealing Midnight's food, she chases him all over the house.

	Bo Derek
TIGER	Charlotte Bronte
	Calvin Coolidge
	Aaron Neville
TIGGER	Stephen Dorff
	Gladys Taber
TIGGY	Red Buttons

Red Buttons uses his cat to choose his comedy material. He puts a different joke on three separate pieces of paper, lets Tiggy choose one with his paw and then throws the other jokes away.

TIMMY'S KITTY	Betty White
TINKER	
	Dame Alicia Markova
	Juliet Prowse
TINKER BELL	
	Waylon Jennings
TINKERBELL	
	Lorraine Bracco
TINO	Taran Noah Smith
TIPPY	Bobby Sherman
TISH	Love Hewitt
TOBASCO	Cokie Roberts
TOBY	Betty White
TOM	Orson Bean
	Roger A. Caras
	Earl Holliman
TOM CAT	Katie Kelly
TOM KITTEN	
	Caroline Kennedy
	Beatrix Potter
TOM QUARTZ	
	Teddy Roosevelt
TOM TERRIFIC	
	John F. Kennedy
TOM, JR.	
	Harriet Beecher Stowe

TOMMY Harvey Korman	VINCENT Vincent Price
TOMORROW	Liz Taylor
Audrey Hepburn	VIRGIL Robert Southey
TOONSES Melissa Gilbert	W.C. FIELDS Ed McMahon
TOP BOY James Mason	WALLY Gertrude Lawrence
TOPAZ Tennessee Williams	WARLORD Orson Bean
TOPBOY Pamela Mason	WEASEL Cyndi Lauper
TOSS Matthew Arnold	WEBSTER P. G. Wodehouse
TOUGH CHARLIE	WEEDON Edward Gorey
Paul Gallico	WEENEY Martha Stewart
TOUGH TOM Paul Gallico	WENDY Orson Bean
TOUNE Colette	WHISPER John Belushi
TRAVIS Doc Severinsen	WHISTLE Marcia Rodd
TREE James Mason	WHITE HEATHER
TRISTAN	Queen Victoria
Catherine Oxenberg	WHITE WICKER
TROT Thomas Hardy	Pamela Mason
TUBBS Yeardley Smith	WHITEHEAD
TUFFY Loni Anderson	Ernest Hemingway
TULA Barbara Baxley	WHITEY James Mason
TUMBLEBRUTUS T. S. Eliot	Pamela Mason
TURKEY Janet Leigh	WILHELMINA
TUT-AZAM Jack Albertson	Charles Dickens
TWO FACE Linda Evans	
TZING-MAO James Taylor	Charles Dickens cat Wil-
VALERIANO WEYLER	helmina craved attention, espe-
William McKinley	cially when Dickens was trying
	to write. If she didn't get it, she
VELVEETA Bill Beyers	would put him into the dark by
VIC VIC Ray Bradbury	putting out his candle with her
	paw.
	WILLIE George Burns

Ed Reingold
David L. Wolper

WIN WIN   Ray Bradbury

WINGLEY
Katherine Mansfield
John Middleton Murray

WINSTON   Lily Tomlin

WISCUS   T. S. Eliot

WOLF   Christopher Walken

WUZZY   Paul Gallico

YANKEE
Dr. William DeVries

YAZ   Ken Burns

ZAK   Amy Stock Poynton

ZAP   Wilt Chamberlain

ZAPATOS   Yeardley Smith

ZARA   Horace Walpole

ZEKE   James Mason

ZELDA   Robert Donner

ZERT   Christina Ricci

ZIGGY   Willard Scott

ZIP   Wilt Chamberlain

ZIZI   Theophile Gautier

ZOBEIDE
Theophile Gautier

ZOMBI   Robert Southey

ZOROASTER   Mark Twain

ZSA ZSA   Eva Gabor

ZULA   James Taylor

ZULEIKA Theophile Gautier

ZULEMA Theophile Gautier

ZUT   Guy Wetmore Carryl

HORSE

NAMES

1.2.3.   Leslie Howard

AARON   D. H. Lawrence

When writer D.H. Lawrence's horse Aaron died, he had his hide made into a duffel bag.

ABASTER   Pluto

ABATOS   Pluto

ABDULLAH
        Benjamin Harrison

ABOVE SUSPICION
        Queen Elizabeth II

ACE   Tim McCoy
                  Tom Tyler

ACK ACK   Greer Garson

AETHE   Agamemnon

AETHON   Apollo
                   Athena
        Hector of Troy
                   Helios

AETON   Pluto

AFTERNOON DELIGHTS
        Burt Bacharach

AGNES
      Mary, Queen of Scots

AJAX   Robert E. Lee

ALAMAIN   Ronald Reagan

ALASTOR   Pluto

ALBORAK   Mohammed

ALDEBARAN   Ben Hur

ALEXANDER
        Queen Elizabeth II

ALGONQUIN
        Teddy Roosevelt

ALI   Napoleon Bonaparte

ALIBHAI   Louis B. Mayer

ALICE-OF-THE-NIGHT
        King Richard the Lion-
                   Hearted

ALLAHMANDE
    General George S. Patton

ALTAIR   Ben Hur

ALTOBELLO
        King Henry VIII

ALYFAR   Arthur Godfrey

AMETHEA   Helios

AMIGO   Robby Benson

ANDY   Budweiser
                   Clara Bow

ANGEL   Bo Derek

ANGELINA   Velvet Brown

ANTARES   Ben Hur

APACHE   Bob Barker
                   Kit Carson
                   Tom Mix

ARAB   Winston Churchill

Arab was the pony that Winston Churchill rode with the Lancers when he was fighting in Egypt as a young officer.

ARABELLE   Hayley Mills

ARION   Hercules

ARTHUR OF TROY
                    Princess Anne

ASHBY   Henry Douglas

ASTRAPE   Helios

AUREOLE
                Queen Elizabeth I

AUSTERLITZ
            Napoleon Bonaparte

BABA   Clark Gable
                Grace Kelly

BABIECA   El Cid

When eleventh century Spanish hero El Cid was killed in battle, his body was lashed upright on his white warhorse Babieca, fooling the enemy into believing that El Cid was still alive.

BABY   Mariah Carey

BALDY
        General George Meade

During the Civil War, the hero of Gettysburg, General George Meade, had Baldy shot out from under him three times, yet the horse survived to lead Meade's funeral procession.

BALIUS   Achilles

BANDIT   Princess Anne
                Prince Charles

BANJO   Lucky Jenkins
                    Tom Mix

BANNER   Bob Steele

BARAKAT   Tyrone Power

BARNUM   Laura Ingalls

BARON   Budweiser
                   Tim McCoy
                    Tom Tyler

BATTLE ROYAL
              Burt Bacharach

BAYARD
        General Philip Kearny

BAZOOKA   Lou Costello

BEAR   Elvis Presley

BEAU   Rooster Cogburn

BEAU PERE   Louis B. Mayer

BEAUREGARD
        General Wade Hampton

BEAUTY   Adam Cartwright
                Joan Crawford
                 Hayley Mills

BELLBOY
             Queen Elizabeth II

BEPPO
        General Judson Kilpatrick

BETSY   Queen Elizabeth II

BETTY   Elizabeth Taylor

BIG NOISE   Betty Grable

BILL   Budweiser

BILLY   Buffalo Bill Cody
                 Thomas Eakin
              Benjamin Harrison
                   Pat Morrow
         Colonel James Penfield
         General George Thomas

BILLY BUTTON
Ulysses Simpson Grant

BLACK BEAUTY   Art Acord

BLACK BESS
General John Hunt Morgan
Dick Turpin

BLACK JACK
General John Logan

BLACK NELL
Wild Bill Hickock

BLACKIE   Chief Sitting Bull

BLACKJACK
John F. Kennedy
Allan "Rocky" Lane

BLANCHARD   Charlemagne

BLANK   Cinderella

BLAZE KING   Velvet Brown

BLEISTEIN   Teddy Roosevelt

BLUE BABY   Lou Costello

BLUESKIN
George Washington

BOB   Abraham Lincoln

BOLD BAZOOKA
Lou Costello

BOLIVIA   Andrew Jackson

BOOMERANG
Eddie Macken

BOOTLEGGER   Will Rogers

BR FEROUK ROBERT
Patrick Swayze

BREMO   Thomas Jefferson

BRIGADIER REX
Edgar Rice Burroughs

BRIGHAM   Buffalo Bill Cody

Buffalo Bill's horse, which was named after Mormon leader Brigham Young, was specially trained by Indians for use in shooting buffalo. In one seventeen month period, Bill killed over four thousand buffalo atop Brigham.

BRIGLIADORE   Sir Guyon

BROADWAY JOE
Bing Crosby

BRONTE   Helios

BROWN BEAUTY
Paul Revere

Paul Revere rode Brown Beauty on his famous Midnight Ride to Lexington and Concord at the start of the American Revolution, in which he alerted the countryside to "be up and to arm." Unfortunately, Brown Beauty was captured, and spent the rest of the war fighting for the British.

BROWN ROAN
Robert E. Lee

BROWNIE   Bob Steele

BRUIN   Sam Houston

BUCEPHALUS
Alexander the Great

Alexander the Great discovered that his horse was

afraid of his own shadow. Since the only way that he could ride him was directly into the sun, when invading towards the east, Alexander had to ensure that battles occurred in the morning.

BUCK   Budweiser
              Ben Cartwright
              Marshal Matt Dillon

BUCKSHOT
              Wild Bill Hickock

BUCKSKIN JOE
              Buffalo Bill Cody

BUD   Edgar Rice Burroughs

BULL REIGH Louis B. Mayer

BULLET   General Jeb Stuart

BURMESE
              Queen Elizabeth II

BURNS
General George B. McClellan

During the Civil War, General George B. McClellan's horse Burns had one dysfunction. When it was time for dinner, he would turn around and head home, even if it was in the middle of a major battle.

BUSHER   Louis B. Mayer

BUSSACO
              Queen Elizabeth II

BUSTER
              Edgar Rice Burroughs

BUTCHER BOY
              Ulysses Simpson Grant

Grant was constantly receiving speeding tickets for racing his horses through the streets of Washington, D.C. Once, he was outrun by a butcher's wagon, so he stopped the peddler and immediately bought his horse, which he dubbed Butcher Boy.

BUTLER
              General Wade Hampton

BUTTERCUP   Bo Derek

BUTTERMILK   Dale Evans

BUTTON   Thomas Paine

CABALL   King Arthur

CACAO   James T. West

CACTUS KATE
              William S. Hart

CALICO   Gabby Hayes

CAPTAIN   Budweiser
              Edgar Rice Burroughs

CARITA   Bo Derek

CARLOS
          Don Hernando De Soto

CATALINA   Ronald Reagan

CELOSA   Bo Derek

CENTAURO   Bo Derek

CENTENNIAL
              Queen Elizabeth II

CHAMPION   Gene Autry

Gene Autry's horse in all of his western films and TV shows was Champion, whose hoofprints are immortalized forever in the cement in front of Mann's Chinese Theatre in Hollywood.

CHANCELLOR	General Jeb Stuart
CHAPEL	Will Rogers
CHARLEY	George Catlin
	William Clarke Quantrill
CHARLIE	
	General Nathaniel Banks
CHINKLING	
	George Washington
CHUB	Hoss Cartwright
CINCINNATUS	
	Ulysses Simpson Grant
CLAVILENO	Don Quixote
CLEOPATRA	John Adams
COCHISE	
	Little Joe Cartwright
COCO	Nick Barkley
	Napoleon Bonaparte
COLA	John Wilkes Booth
COLONEL	
	Edgar Rice Burroughs
COLUMBUS	Princess Anne
	Queen Elizabeth II
COMANCHE	
	Captain Myles Keogh

Captain Myles Keogh's horse Comanche was the only survivor of Custer's Last Stand at the Battle of the Little Big Horn in 1876, surviving as an honored member of the 7th Cavalry until 1891. He received his name in his first military action, when he was wounded by a Comanche arrow.

	Tom Mix
	Will Rogers
COMET	Supergirl
	Briscoe County, Jr.
COMMANDER	Budweiser
COND	
	Frederick the Great
CONQUISTADOR	
	Leo Carrillo
COPENHAGEN	
	Duke of Wellington
COPPER	Eddie Dean
CORASON	Bo Derek
CORPORAL	Bo Derek
COSA RARA	
	King Ludwig II of Bavaria
COSSACK	
	Queen Elizabeth II
COWBOY	Will Rogers
CREOLE	Robert E. Lee
CROW	
	Edgar Rice Burroughs

CUBA — Will Rogers

CUSTIS LEE
  George Armstrong Custer

CYROCK — Jesse James

DAN — Frank James

DANDY
  George Armstrong Custer

DANIEL WEBSTER
General George B. McClellan

DANSEUSE
        Jacqueline Onassis

DAPPLE — Sancho Panza

DEAN — Budweiser

DECATUR
  General Philip Kearny

DENNIS — Charles Bronson
        Jill Ireland

DESIREE
        Napoleon Bonaparte

DIABLO — Cisco Kid
        Duncan Renaldo

DICE — Gene Autry

DICK
  General Ambrose Burnside

DIOMEDE
        Thomas Jefferson

DOBBIN — Dirk Bogarde

DODO — Will Rogers

DOLL OF ALBUQUERQUE
        Bo Derek

DOLLY — Gen. William-
        Tecumseh Sherman

George Washington

DOMINO — Priscilla Presley

DON JUAN
  George Armstrong Custer

DON'T–STOP–THE–MUSIC
        Cubby Broccoli

DOPEY — Will Rogers

DOT — Eleanor Roosevelt

DOUBLET — Princess Anne

DOUTELLE
        Queen Elizabeth II

DUKE — Budweiser
        Tim Holt
        John Wayne
        James T. West

EAGLE — Thomas Jefferson

EARLY BIRD — Fred Astaire

EBENEZER — Chief Joseph

EBONY
  General Benjamin Butler
        Arthur Miller
        Marilyn Monroe

EGYPT
  Ulysses Simpson Grant

EL MORZILLO
        Hernando Cortez

  Spanish Conquistador Hernando Cortez's horse El Morzillo was injured while he was conquering Mexico. Cortez left him in Guatemala with Mayans who promptly adopted him as their god, worshiped him until he died, and then erected a statue in his honor.

EMILY   Andrew Jackson

EMMINE
          Mary Frances Crosby

EOA   Helios

ESBAN   Dorothy Squires

ETHON   Hector

EXCELSIOR
          General Nelson Miles

FABULOUS NOTION
                      Ray Stark

FACT FINDER
          Nelson B. Hunt

FADDA   Mohammed

FALCON   Buster Crabbe

FANCY   Velvet Brown

FANNIE
     General Joseph Johnston

FATIMA
          Martha Washington

Martha Washington is not as sedate as most historians would paint her. When she was a little girl she rode her horse Fatima up the stairs of her parents' house.

FATUSHKA   Zsa Zsa Gabor

FAUVEL
          King Richard the Lion-
                      Hearted

FIDELITY   Ethel Roosevelt

FIRE-EATER
     General Albert Johnston

FIREFLY
     General Isaac Sherwood

FLASH   Gary Cooper
                    Eddie Dean

FLICKA   Ken McLaughlin

FLORIDA   Bo Derek

FLY   Alonzo "Manly" Wilder

FLYING JOHN
                    Audie Murphy

FOX   Ulysses Simpson Grant

FRANCIS   Peter Sterling

FRED ASTAIRE
                    Jock Whitney

FRITZ   William S. Hart

FRU-FRU   Benito Mussolini

FUBUKI   Emperor Hirohito

FURY   Joey Newton

FYVIE   Queen Victoria

GALATHE   Hector

GAMBLING BLUE
                      Bo Derek

GATO   Aime Felix Tschiffely

GENERAL   Teddy Roosevelt
          General Jeb Stuart
          President John Tyler

GEORGE   Velvet Brown

GLEN KATE   Wayne Gretzky

GLENCOE
     General John Hunt Morgan

GOBO   John Cromwell

GOLDEN BOY JET
                Jennie Garth

GOLDIE   Hoot Gibson
                Arthur Godfrey

GOODWILL   Princess Anne

GOVERNATORE
                King Henry VIII

GRACE DARLING
                Robert E. Lee

GRADUATE   Katharine Ross

GRAY GHOST
                Chief Sitting Bull
                Buffalo Bill Cody

GREY DAWN
                Teddy Roosevelt

GUALIANKO
                Ronald Reagan

GUAPO   Bo Derek

GUNPOWDER
                Ichabod Crane

HAIL COLUMBUS
                Harvey Korman

Harvey Korman, even though he loves horses, felt he had overpaid for Hail Columbus, and was overjoyed when Tim Conway showed up with a buyer. They had already agreed on a price, when the buyer's daughter said she didn't like the color. Harvey immitately piped up with "We'll paint him."

HARARA
                Edgar Rice Burroughs

HARRY
    George Armstrong Custer
                John Mitchum
                Robert Mitchum

HATSUSHIMO
                Emperor Hirohito

HEARTLIGHT NO. ONE
                Burt Bacharach
                Neil Diamond

Burt Bacharach, with Carole Bayer Sager and Neil Diamond, named their champion filly after the trio's hit song, "Heartlight." As stated by Burt, "My misfortune was to have my first horse, Battle Royal, win my first race. I had the No. 1 and No. 4 songs in the country, but that didn't compare with that feeling."

                Carole Bayer Sager

HELMUT   Bo Derek

HEMISPHERE
                Louis B. Mayer

HERO   Phantom
    General James Longstreet

HI HO SILVER   Bo Derek

HIGH JINKS   Princess Anne

HIGH SKY
                General Jeb Stuart

HIGH VELDT
                Queen Elizabeth II

HONEYMOON
Louis B. Mayer

HOUDINI   Bo Derek

IMPERIAL
Queen Elizabeth II

INCITATUS   Caligula

Caligula the mad emperor of Rome, worshiped his horse, whom he often let serve as the host at his parties. Incitatus had a marble manger, an ivory stall, and a host of slaves who served him water in a goblet of solid gold. Caligula made him a senator and priest.

INDIAN WOMAN
David Carradine

IRON MAIDEN
Louis B. Mayer

ISHAM   Buffalo Bill Cody

ISMAEL
Ulysses Simpson Grant

JACK
Ulysses Simpson Grant

U.S. Grant's horse Jack was a cream-colored stallion who was so conspicuous that Grant couldn't ride him on the battlefield, so he donated him to an auction that was raising money for wounded veterans.

Sam Houston
George Washington

George Washington's horse Jack was bought by promoter John Bill Ricketts, and became a sideshow attraction in America's first circus.

JACK RUCKER
George Armstrong Custer

JACKSON
George Washington

JADAN
Dr. Harvey Kellogg
Rudolph Valentino

JAFFA   Napoleon Bonaparte

JAKE   Budweiser

JAKLIN KLUGMAN
Jack Klugman

"Jaklin, my wonderful horse, came into my life at a time when I needed him most," Jack Klugman once said. "I get up at 4:30 in the morning and go to the racetrack to watch my horse . . . eat hay. I just sit for an hour and just watch him eat hay. The biggest thrill of my life was when he won the California Derby. Emmys are nice, but this is my idea of excitement."

JASPER   Tom Mix

JEFF
General John J. Pershing

JEFF DAVIS
Ulysses Simpson Grant

As the North became more successful in the Civil War, and invaded the South, one of the plantations that was captured was that of Confederacy President Jefferson Davis. General Grant convinced one of Davis' ponies, which he dubbed Jeff Davis, to fight for the Union, and it became one of his favorite mounts until long after the war was over.

JENNIE
    Ulysses Simpson Grant

JENNY GEDDES
    Robert Burns

JIM   Robert E. Lee
    John Mitchum
    Robert Mitchum

JOCK   King George V

JOCKO   Teddy Roosevelt

JOHN   Benjamin Harrison

JOHN COLTER
    Katharine Ross

JOHNNY'S IMAGE
    David Cassidy

JOLLY   George Washington

JUDGE   Olivia Newton-John
    Teddy Roosevelt

JUDGE ANGELUCCI
    Nelson B. Hunt

JULIA
    Ulysses Simpson Grant

K-DOC   Charles Bronson
    Jill Ireland

KANGAROO
    Ulysses Simpson Grant

KANTHAKA   Buddha

KATIE   Emmet Dalton
    Jesse James

KAWALEER   Bo Derek

KENTUCKY   Jefferson Davis

KIDRON
    General John J. Pershing

KILDARE   King Edward VII

KING   Edgar Rice Burroughs
    Bill Cody

KING JOHN
    Marlene Dietrich

KING PHILLIP
    Nathan Bedford Forrest

KING WOODFORD
    Tom Mix

KIT   James A. Garfield

KO-KO   Rex Allen

LADY LEE   Jimmy Carter

LADY LIKE   Bo Derek

LADY NASHVILLE
    Andrew Jackson

LAMRI   King Arthur

LE SOLARET
    Burt Bacharach
    Neil Diamond
    Carole Bayer Sager

LEONIDAS   Robert E. Lee
            George Washington

LEOPARD
    Ulysses Simpson Grant

LEPRECHAUN
        John F. Kennedy, Jr.

LETAN
        Edgar Rice Burroughs

LEXINGTON
            Benjamin Harrison
            Gen. William-
            Tecumseh Sherman

LIGAROTI   Bing Crosby

Bing Crosby was the driving force behind the creation of the Del Mar racetrack, just north of San Diego, California. Crosby's voice is still heard crooning the song *Where the Turf Meets the Surf* at the beginning and end of every race day.

LIGHTNING   Tim Holt

LINDEN TREE
        Ulysses Simpson Grant

LINDY   Gene Autry

LITTLE JOHN   Slim Pickens

LITTLE KING
            Yvonne De Carlo

LITTLE MAN Ronald Reagan

LOCHNAGAR
            Queen Victoria

LOCO   Pancho

LOLLY C.   Lou Costello

LOOKOUT
    General Joseph Hooker

LOUCOUNI   Robert Wagner

LUCKY   Clara Bow
                 Dick West

LUCY
    General George Pickett

LUNA DARLING   Bo Derek

LYARD   King Richard the
                 Lion-Hearted

MACARONI
            Caroline Kennedy

MADAME LA REALE
        Mary, Queen of Scots

MAGIC   Brooke Shields

MAGNOLIA
Gen."Light Horse" Harry Lee
            George Washington

George Washington was first in war, first in peace, and first in the hearts of his countrymen, but not always first in horseracing. His horse Magnolia lost to Thomas Jefferson's roan colt in 1788, and Washington sold him.

MAHMOUD   Aga Khan

MAJOR   Cinderella
    General Ambrose Burnside

MAMSELLE BEBETTE
            John Forsythe

MANCHO
Aime Felix Tschiffely

MANITOU
Teddy Roosevelt

MARENGO
Napoleon Bonaparte

MARIE
Napoleon Bonaparte

MARK   Budweiser

MARY
Ulysses Simpson Grant

MARYLAND
General Jeb Stuart

MAUD S.
Ulysses Simpson Grant

MCKINLEY
Buffalo Bill Cody

MEHEYL   Mike Nichols

MELODY   Clark Gable

MERCURY   Bo Derek

MIDNIGHT   Tim McCoy

MIKE   George O'Brien

MISS ADA   Velvet Brown

MISS LONG   Robert E. Lee

MISTER ED   Anne McCaffrey
              Wilbur Post

MISTY GIRL   Victoria Barkley

MOCHA BAILEY
Drew Barrymore

MONARCH   Queen Victoria

MONMOUTH
General Philip Kearny

MONTE   Charles Russell

MONTE BLACK   Will Rogers

MOONLIGHT   Tyrone Power

MOSCOW
General Philip Kearny

MOURITO   Bo Derek

MOURO   Bo Derek

MR. DINKUM   Prince Andrew

MRS. JAMES   Velvet Brown

MUSON   Buffalo Bill Cody

MUTT   Hoot Gibson

MYSORE   Bo Derek

NAPOLEON
General Winfield Scott

NELLIE GRAY
General Fitzhugh Lee

NELSON
George Washington

George Washington's horse Nelson was his favorite battle charger, which he rode on the day he accepted the surrender of General Cornwallis at Yorktown, the battle which won the American Revolution.

NEUADD HILLSIDE
Jack London

NEW DEAL
Franklin Delano Roosevelt

NO STRINGS   Nancy Reagan

OLD BLUE   Tom Mix

When Tom Mix decided to

leave Oklahoma to become a star in Hollywood, he only had enough money for him and his faithful steed Old Blue to take the train as far as San Bernardino. Flat broke, he had to ride Old Blue the rest of the way to Hollywood.

OLD BOB   Abraham Lincoln

OLD CHARLIE
            Buffalo Bill Cody

OLD DOMINION
            Shannen Doherty

OLD PETE   Sam Houston

OLD ROWLEY
            King Charles II

OLD SMOKY
            Buffalo Bill Cody

OLD SORREL
  General Stonewall Jackson

OLD SPOT   William Kellogg

OLD WHITEY
            Zachary Taylor

Zachary Taylor captured Old Whitey from a Mexican officer during the Mexican War in 1847, and when he became President let him graze on the White House lawn. Old Whitey survived Taylor to pull his hearse, was drafted in 1861, survived military service in the Civil War and was then able to finally retire out to pasture.

OVER ANXIOUS
            Fred Astaire

PADDY
            Captain Myles Keogh

PAINT   Tonto

PAINTED BEIL
            Louis B. Mayer

PAL   Gene Autry
                  Dale Evans
                  Tim McCoy

PAPPY   Christina Crawford

PARDNER   Monte Hall
                  Al Hoxie

PASSE BREWELL
            Sir Tristram

PATCHES   Eve Arden

PATTY   Charles Ingalls

PEACOCK
      Junius Brutus Booth

PECOS   Wrangler Jane

PEGASUS   Apollo
   Major Charles Emerson
            Winchester III

PEPPER   Jack Lemmon
               Johnny Nelson

PET   Charles Ingalls

PHANTOM   Zorro

PHIL SHERIDAN
   George Armstrong Custer

PHLEGON   Apollo

PIE   Velvet Brown

      Elizabeth Taylor played

Velvet Brown in the classic film *National Velvet*, riding to victory on her horse Pie, who in real life was a horse named King Charles, a grandson of the famous Man O' War. Liz was so in love with the horse that the studio gave it to her for her 14th birthday.

POCO LEO	Bo Derek
PODARGUS	Hector
POKEY	Gumby
PONCA	Tom Mix
POWIS CASTLE	Berry Gordy
PRIDE	Princess Anne
PRINCE	Buffalo Bill Cody
PSYCHE	Charles Bronson Jill Ireland
PUMPERNICKEL	Napoleon Bonaparte
PURGATORY	Dustin Farnum
PURPLE STAR	Princess Anne
PYROIS	Apollo
RAIDER	Durango Kid
RAINBOW TIE	Fred Astaire
RANGER	Roy Stewart George Washington
RAWHIDE	Range Rider
RAZOR	Lucas McCain
REB	Ulysses Simpson Grant
REBEL	Johnny Mack Brown
RED BUCK	Emmet Dalton
RED FOX	Jesse James
RENOWN	Teddy Roosevelt
REX	Monte Montana Sergeant William Preston
RICHMOND	Robert E. Lee
RIENZI	General Phil Sheridan
RIGEL	Ben Hur
RINGO	Steve McQueen
RISING SUN	Elvis Presley
RIVLIA	Nelson B. Hunt
ROAN BARBARY	King Richard II
ROANOKE	George Armstrong Custer
ROBBIE	Charles Bronson Jill Ireland
ROBIN	Abraham Lincoln Will Rogers

Will Rogers loved this large red sorrel with a flaxen mane and tail which had been stolen from its former master by a famous outlaw, Cherokee Bill, who was later hung at Fort Smith, Arkansas. Will liked the horse because Cherokee Bill had trained the horse so well to help him get out of scrapes. Robin's tricks included jumping fences and swimming rivers.

ROCKY
 Kermit "Tex" Maynard

ROITELET
 Napoleon Bonaparte

ROLLA
 General Winfield Scott

RONALD Lord Cardigan

Lord Cardigan, famous for his Charge of the Light Brigade during the Crimean War upon his horse Ronald, later went on to invent the cardigan sweater.

ROOT Teddy Roosevelt

ROSABELLA
 Mary, Queen of Scots

ROSINANTE Don Quixote

ROSWELL Teddy Roosevelt

ROWENA Lana Turner

ROYAL GIFT
 George Washington

ROZINANTE
 George Washington

RUSH Lash LaRue

RUSSIA'S MOON Bo Derek

RUSTY Teddy Roosevelt

RUTH Festus Haggen

SAM
 Gen. William-Tecumseh Sherman

SAM PATCHES
 Andrew Jackson

SAMMY Budweiser

SAMSON
 George Washington

SAN QUININA
 Prince Charles

SANTA ANNA
 Robert E. Lee

SARDAR
 Jacqueline Onassis

SAVOY King Charles VIII

SCAR Britt Ponset

SCOUT Tonto
 Jack Hoxie

SEAN Hayley Mills

SHARAD-NAR-AL-DIN
 Tamarlane
 Timur

SHENANDOAH
 General Nathaniel Banks

SILVER Sunset Carson
 Buck Jones
 Lone Ranger

SILVER BULLET
 Whip Wilson

SILVER FOX Zsa Zsa Gabor

SILVER KING Fred Thomson

SIR PERICLES Velvet Brown

SIROC Jesse James

SKIP Laura Ingalls

SKYLARK
General Jeb Stuart

SLEIPNER Odin

SLICK Bo Derek

SLIP ALONG Spencer Tracy

SMOKEY Kid Shaleen

SNOWFLAKE Texas Guinan

SO SHE SLEEPS
Albert Finney

SOAPSUDS Will Rogers

SOLDIER BOY
Buffalo Bill Cody

SOLE OF THE MATTER
Burt Bacharach

SOMBRA Prince Charles

SONNY Bill Elliott

SOPHIE
Colonel Sherman Potter

SPUMADOR King Arthur

SPUNKY Shirley Temple

Shirley Temple was so enamored with the horse that she rode in her film *Curly Top*, that the studio gave it to her.

ST. LOUIS
Ulysses Simpson Grant

STAR OF THE EAST
General Jeb Stuart

STARLIGHT Hoot Gibson
Bob Livingston
Tim McCoy
Jack Perrin

STEADY
George Washington

STEAMBOAT
Buffalo Bill Cody
Daniel Webster

Daniel Webster buried his favorite horse Steamboat with his halter and shoes on, standing upright in his grave.

STEED Dudley Do-Right

STEVE'S FRIEND
George Steinbrenner

STHENIUS Poseidon

STORMY
Gordon "Wild Bill" Elliot

STRIPE Bo Derek

STRYMON Xerxes

SULTAN Queen Elizabeth II

SULTAN'S GREAT DAY
William Shatner

William Shatner's horse Sultan's Great Day was featured in the book *Vavra's Horses* as one of the ten most beautiful horses in the world.

SUN BRANDY
Wayne Gretzky

SUNDOWN Will Rogers

SUNNY Barry Goldwater

SUNSET Jimmy Wakely

SYLVESTER
Professor Marvel

TAGGART Tom Mix

TALL BULL
Buffalo Bill Cody

Before Buffalo Bill started his Wild West Show, he was an Indian fighter. In a battle with Cheyenne war chief Tall Bull, he killed the chief, captured his horse, and named it after him.

TAMERLANE   William Penn

TANYA TUCKER   Bo Derek

TARGA   John Forsythe

TARGET   Annie Oakley

TARTAR   Jefferson Davis
Queen Victoria

TARZAN   Bo Derek
Ken Maynard

TAURIS
Napoleon Bonaparte

TECUMSEH
Thomas Jefferson

TEDDY   Will Rogers

TELLY'S POP   Telly Savalas

When Telly learned that his horse had won an award at the racetrack, he immediately left the set of *Kojak*, even though the producer said it would personally cost Telly $5,000 a minute. Telly didn't care. He said he didn't need show business any more, this was a bigger thrill.

TENCENDUR
Charlemagne

TEX   Caroline Kennedy

THE DOLT   El Cid

THUNDER   Phantom
Red Ryder

THUNDERBOLT
Johnny West

THUNDERHEAD
Ken McLaughlin

TILBURY   Queen Elizabeth I

TIME MACHINE
William Shatner

TONY   Tom Mix

TONY, JR.   Gene Autry
Tom Mix

TOPPER   Hopalong Cassidy

TORNADO   Zorro

TRAVELLER
Winston Churchill
Robert E. Lee
George Washington

TRIGGER   Roy Rogers

Roy Rogers named his famous sidekick Trigger because he was so smart and so fast, he was "quick on the trigger." Trigger's hoofprints are in the cement in front of Mann's Chinese Theatre in Hollywood.

TRIPLICATE   Fred Astaire

TRIXY   Laura Ingalls

TRUXTON   Andrew Jackson

Andrew Jackson was heavily in debt, so he purchased Truxton, a racehorse, and ran him in a famous race against Greyhound. His profits from this race made him solvent, and enabled him to go on and become President.

TWO BITS Johnny Crawford

TWO SOCKS   Spencer Tracy

VALKYRIE   Prince Andrew

VEILLANTIFF   Roland

VENTURA   Bo Derek

VENUS   Belle Starr

VIC

George Armstrong Custer

The horse that General Custer was riding at the Battle of Little Big Horn in 1876 was Vic, and he died fighting the Indians with his master.

VIRGINIA
            General Jeb Stuart

VIZIR   Napoleon Bonaparte

WAGRAM
            Napoleon Bonaparte

WARREN
    General Benjamin Butler

WASHINGTON
        General Winfield Scott

WASHOE BAN
            Jack London

Jack London's favorite riding horse was Washoe Ban. In 1906, after the great San Francisco earthquake, he rode him to watch the city burn down in the great fire which followed.

WEE WILLIE WINKIE
            Mary Hayley Bell

WELLINGTON
            Thomas Jefferson

WHISKEY JACK
        Edgar Rice Burroughs

WHITE CLOUD Eddie Dean

WHITE EAGLE   Buck Jones

WHITE FELLER   Tonto

WHITE FLASH   Tex Ritter

WHITE FURY   Jack Hoxie

WHITE SURREY
            King Richard III

King Richard III, when he was afoot in battle and yelled, "A horse, a horse, my kingdom for a horse," had fallen from White Surrey.

WHITEY   Hoot Gibson

WIDOW-MAKER   Pecos Bill

WINCHESTER
        General Phil Sheridan

WINSTON
            Queen Elizabeth II

WYOMING Teddy Roosevelt

XANTHUS   Achilles

	Hector
YAGENKA	Teddy Roosevelt
ZOMBIE	Bing Crosby

UNIQUE

PETS

ALLIGATOR

FRED   Burt Reynolds

ANTELOPE

LEONIE   Albert Schweitzer

Dr. Albert Schweitzer's antelope Leonie lived in his bedroom, where he would wreak havoc when the doctor was out doing good, eating his notes and shredding his clothes.

BABOON

JOU JOO   Leonore Brandt

BADGER

JOSIAH   Teddy Roosevelt

BEAR

BROWNIE   Nell Shipman

FAIRCHILD
            Elly May Clampett

JONATHAN EDWARDS
            Teddy Roosevelt

ROCKY
   General Maxwell D. Taylor

SMOKEY   US Forest Service

BENGAL TIGER

ZAZU   Tippi Hedren

BIRD

BOZO
         Mary Kate McGeehan

CHARLIE   Tori Spelling

GAYLORD
            Tallulah Bankhead

Tallulah Bankhead's bird Gaylord had a great trick. He would untie the shoelaces of the male guests who came to her house.

GOLDY   Calvin Coolidge

JOEY   Doris Day

WOODSTOCK
            Snoopy the Dog

BOA CONSTRICTOR

ANGEL   Alice Cooper

BO   Brian Austin Green

FRED   Jermaine Jackson

MUSCLES   Janet Jackson

MUSCLES   Michael Jackson

Frank Dileo, the promotions director at Epic Records, was deadly afraid of boa constrictors. As a child, Michael Jackson knew this, and used to delight in holding Muscles over his head and chasing Frank around the soundstage.

BOBCAT

SMOKY   Calvin Coolidge

Calvin Coolidge was reluctant to accept Smoky, a wild bobcat sent to him when he was President. However, he didn't dare send it back, because it came from a solidly Republican county in Tennessee.

BULL

RED CAP 190   Steve Reeves

CAMEL

AL KASWA   Mohammed

CANARY

DICKIE
          Edgar Rice Burroughs

JOHNNY TY
          President John Tyler

NIP   Calvin Coolidge

ROBIN   John F. Kennedy

SNOWFLAKE
          Calvin Coolidge

TUCK   Calvin Coolidge

CHEETAH

KENYA   Gardner McKay

PHARAOH   Tippi Hedren

RHETT BUTLER
          Tippi Hedren

SCARLETT O'HARA
          Tippi Hedren

CHICKEN

Betty   Glenn Ford

Glenn Ford raised chickens in the backyard of his Beverly Hills home. The Beverly Hills city authorities gave him a hard time, until he pointed out that his neighbor and good friend Rita Hayworth didn't object to the chickens, and his other neighbor Dinah Shore didn't complain when he gave her a couple of dozen eggs a week.

CHICKEN CHILD
          Nanette Fabray

Nanette Fabray had a pet chicken that she dubbed Chicken Child who was thrown out of the nest by her mother because she thought that the chick was defective. The chick became a house pet, and Nanette tried to teach it how to do chicken things, only to come to the realization that his mother was right, and the chicken was not all that bright.

FELIX   Michael Gray

CHIMPANZEE

A.J.   Michael Jackson

BUBBLES   Michael Jackson

CHEETAH   Tarzan

COUSIN BESS
          Elly May Clampett

FIFI   Dr. Jane Goodall

GOBLIN   Dr. Jane Goodall

MAX   Michael Jackson

CHINESE CHICKEN

BILLY IDOL   Kirstie Alley

CHIPMUNK

NIBBLES   Elizabeth Taylor

COCKATIEL

CRUISE	Le Var Burton
GREGORY	Fred Astaire

Fred Astaire called his cockatiel Gregory because he "pecked."

COCKATOO

FRED	Baretta
DUDLEY	Ricki Lake

COW

ELSIE	Gail Borden
HENRY	Alec Baldwin Kim Basinger
MOOLY WOOLY	William Howard Taft
SUKEY	William Henry Harrison

DEER

PRINCE	Michael Jackson
PRINCESS	Michael Jackson

DONKEY

CORNICHOO	Brigitte Bardot
EBENEZER	Calvin Coolidge
LUCIUS	Mai Zetterling
MOLLIE BEE	Eve Arden

DOVE

JULIO	Shannen Doherty
PALOMO	Shannen Doherty
PISSARO	Shannen Doherty

ELEPHANT

GYPSY	Michael Jackson
JUMBO	P. T. Barnum

Jumbo became the most famous elephant in history because his owner, showman P.T. Barnum, created unprecedented hype around his large size, so much so that his name in the English language now means anything "extra big," like jumbo hamburgers and jumbo drinks.

KURA	Tippi Hedren
TIMBO	Tippi Hedren

FAWN

IP	Audrey Hepburn

Audrey Hepburn was very fond of her little deer Ip, and just like Mary and the little lamb, it followed her everywhere.

FINCH

PETEY	Penny Marshall

FISH

BUTCH	Larry Hankin
DIME	Larry Hankin
FROG	Larry Hankin
NICKLE	Larry Hankin
PENNY	Larry Hankin
SEXY	Jenna Von Oy
SILVER	Corey Feldman

THE WONDER FISH
Larry Hankin

GIRAFFE

JABBAR   Michael Jackson

GOAT

DEWEY'S GOAT
Harry S. Truman

ESMERALDA   Pablo Picasso

HIS WHISKERS
William Henry Harrison

NANKO   Abraham Lincoln

NANNY   Abraham Lincoln

Lincoln's goats were treated like members of the family. When a presidential aide suggested that the goats shouldn't ride in the carriage, the aide ended up walking, and the goats rode in style with Lincoln.

NAPOLEON   Earl Holliman

OLD WHISKERS
Benjamin Harrison

GOLDFISH

BIF   Suzanne Somers

MUFFY   Suzanne Somers

GOOSE

ENOCH   Calvin Coolidge

GORILLA

DIGIT   Dian Fossey

KING KONG   Fay Wray

GRIZZLY BEAR

BEN   Grizzly Adams

GUINEA PIG

BISHOP DOAN
Teddy Roosevelt

BOB EVANS
Teddy Roosevelt

CROKED COCONUT
Robert F. Kennedy

DAISY   June Havoc
Gypsy Rose Lee

DEWEY JUNIOR
Teddy Roosevelt

DEWEY SENIOR
Teddy Roosevelt

DR. JOHNSON
Teddy Roosevelt

FATHER O'GRADY
Teddy Roosevelt

JIMMY   June Havoc
Gypsy Rose Lee

SAMBA   June Havoc
Gypsy Rose Lee

SAMBO   June Havoc
Gypsy Rose Lee

HAMSTER

BILLY   John F. Kennedy

BORIS   Luci Johnson

DEBBIE   John F. Kennedy

HEN

BARON SPRECKLE
Teddy Roosevelt

HOG

FLOREINE
    Edgar Rice Burroughs

MARIMOOR PEER
    Edgar Rice Burroughs

HOLSTEIN COW

PAULINE WAYNE
    William Howard Taft

The last first cow, Pauline grazed on the White House lawn and each day, her personal handler delivered her milk directly to the president.

HORNED TOAD

BILL   Teddy Roosevelt

IGUANA

GARFUNKEL   Willie Aames

IGGY   Shelley Duvall

MR. AVA GARDNER
    Tennessee Williams

SIMON   Willie Aames

STIGGY   Shelley Duvall

STUTZ   Shelley Duvall

TWIGGY   Shelley Duvall

LAMB

ORPHAN ANNIE
    Eve Arden

LAMB PUPPET

LAMB CHOP   Shari Lewis

LEOPARD

BUSTER   Tippi Hedren

CLEOPATRA   Tippi Hedren

MARIAH   Tippi Hedren

PEPPER   Tippi Hedren

LION

ALICE   Tippi Hedren

ANTA-M-NEKHT
    Pharaoh Rameses II

BACCHUS   Tippi Hedren

BERRIES   Tippi Hedren

BILLY   Tippi Hedren

BOOMER   Tippi Hedren

BRIDGET   Tippi Hedren

BRUTUS   Tippi Hedren

CASEY   Melanie Griffith

Tippi Hedren, star of Alfred Hitchcock's *The Birds*, built a large ranch which she stocked with lions, tigers, leopards, elephants and cheetahs. Her daughter, future superstar actress Melanie Griffith, regularly slept with the lions, and while she was sleeping with their lion Casey, she couldn't understand why he suddenly bit her!

CHEERIES   Tippi Hedren

CHELSEA   Tippi Hedren

CINDI   Tippi Hedren

DEBBIE   Tippi Hedren

ELSA   Joy Adamson

FRANKIE   Tippi Hedren

GILLIGAN	Tippi Hedren
IGOR	Tippi Hedren
IKE	Tippi Hedren
JACKIE	Metro Goldwyn Mayer
JENNY	Tippi Hedren
JOHNNY	Tippi Hedren
KATRINA	Tippi Hedren
KEMO	Amanda Blake
LENA	Tippi Hedren
LEO	Metro Goldwyn Mayer
LILLIAN	Tippi Hedren
LURCH	Tippi Hedren
MELANIE	Tippi Hedren
MERRIE	Tippi Hedren
MIKE	Tippi Hedren
NANCY	Tippi Hedren
NEEDRA	Tippi Hedren
NEIL	Melanie Griffith
NERO	Tippi Hedren
NOELLE	Tippi Hedren
PARTNER	Melanie Griffith
PENNY	Tippi Hedren
ROBBIE, JR.	Tippi Hedren
SCARFACE	Tippi Hedren
SHELIA	Tippi Hedren
SIMBA	Michael Jackson
TOGAR	Tippi Hedren
TONGARU	Tippi Hedren
TRANS	Tippi Hedren
WINSTON CHURCHILL	Tallulah Bankhead
ZURU	Tippi Hedren

LLAMA

LOLA	Michael Jackson
LOUIS	Michael Jackson

LOBSTER

SPIKE	Mary Tyler Moore

When Mary Tyler Moore learned that Gladstone's Restaurant had a 62-year-old lobster in their tank, she led a successful crusade to save him from being eaten for dinner. When Mary Tyler Moore was trying to save Spike, Rush Limbaugh offered $2,000 to have him for dinner.

MACAW

ELI YALE	Teddy Roosevelt
MOWGLI	Shelley Duvall
SCARLEY-WHARLEY	Shelley Duvall

MOCKINGBIRD

DICK	Thomas Jefferson

MONKEY

BAD BOY	Mae West

When Mae West was looking at diamonds in her limo, the salesman suddenly realized he couldn't find one of the stones he was showing her. Panic stricken, he started searching the entire auto to no avail. Then, Mae noticed that Bad Boy was chewing on something, and opened the monkey's mouth to reveal the diamond.

CHICO	Errol Flynn
CREATURE	Tennessee Williams
KING KONG	Tallulah Bankhead
	Lionel Barrymore
SENEGAS	Tallulah Bankhead

MOUSE

AMOS	Benjamin Franklin

MYNAH BIRD

CLEO	Tallulah Bankhead

OTTER

BUMPY	Tony Dow
OLLIE	Tony Dow

OX

BABE	Paul Bunyan

PARAKEET

BLUEBELL	John F. Kennedy
BUTCH	Arthur Miller
ERNIE	Jonathan Brandis
FIGARO	Michael Gray
MAYBELLE	John F. Kennedy
POCAHONTAS	Vincent Price
ROSIE	Aaron Spelling
TWEETIE	Susan Dey
WOODSTOCK	Betty White

PARROT

ALVIN	Elizabeth Taylor
ANGUS	Bo Derek
AUSTIN	Shelley Duvall
BIG SAL	Robin Williams
CAPTAIN FLINT	Long John Silver
CHARLES A. GREENE	Vincent Price
CHARLIE	David Hasselhoff
CINDY	Mike Vitar
CONNIE	Shelley Duvall
GORBY	Shelley Duvall
GRACIE	Governor Ann Richards
HUMPTY	Shelley Duvall
LAURITA	Tennessee Williams
PERCY	Alec Guinness

Alec Guinness' parrot Percy could recite "O, what a rogue and peasant slave am I."

PETE	Ed Asner
POLLY	Greta Garbo

Greta Garbo's parrot, Polly, would always yell out "Hello, Greta!" when she would enter the room. With no fear of felines, he enjoyed stealing the kitten's food, and then he would give them the raspberry.

POOR POLL
> Andrew Jackson

As with other presidential names, Poll's name soon entered the lexicon of American words as synonymous with parrot. Jackson was devoted to his feathery friend, and when he died, Poll attended the funeral, screaming obscenities at the mourners.

SUNNY   Shelley Duvall

WALL STREET
> T. Boone Pickens

WASHINGTON POST
> William McKinley

William McKinley thought that his yellow parrot Washington Post was the most intelligent animal ever to reside in the White House, because he could finish any song. Among his favorites were *Yankee Doodle* and *America*. McKinley would start to hum, sing or whistle a song, stop, and the parrot would finish it.

PEACOCK

SPRING   Michael Jackson

WINTER   Michael Jackson

☙ Unique Pets' Names

PENGUIN

MILES   Tony Dow

PIEBALD RAT

JONATHAN
> Teddy Roosevelt

PIG

ALEXANDER   Earl Holliman

ARNOLD   Fred Ziffel

MAUDE   Teddy Roosevelt

MAX   George Clooney
> Kelly Preston

PIG   Abraham Lincoln

Abraham Lincoln had a pet pig which he called Pig, and which he used to ride around like a horse.

PIGLET   Christopher Robin

PIGEON

HOMER   Elly May Clampett

WALTER   Earl Holliman

POSSUM

MR. PROTECTION
> Benjamin Harrison

MR. RECIPROCITY
> Benjamin Harrison

RABBIT

BOBBY   Kelly Emberg

FASADINI   Donna Drake

PETER   Teddy Roosevelt

SNOWBALL
> Zachary Ty Bryan

SPEEDY   Kelly Emberg

THUMPER   Fred Astaire

TINY   Maxwell Knight

ZSA ZSA   John F. Kennedy

Zsa Zsa was described by Press Secretary Pierre Salinger as being able to drink beer and then play a toy trumpet, making this rabbit the smartest, and the most talented, of the pets in the Kennedy White House.

RACCOON

HORACE   Calvin Coolidge

RACKY   Elly May Clampett

REBECCA   Calvin Coolidge

RUSSELL   Marlon Brando

Marlon Brando was crazy about his raccoon Russell. He would lead him around on a leash, feed him with a baby bottle, sleep with him and even whispered to him in his sleep.

RAM

MR. TIBBS Michael Jackson

OLD IKE   Woodrow Wilson

Wilson thought that a herd of sheep on the White House lawn would remove the need for gardeners to cut the grass, and the leader of Woodrow's herd was a tobacco chewing ram named Old Ike. Addicted to the nicotine, he would pester the president for a wad, and then calmly stand there and enjoy the chaw, spitting out the juice just like a human.

RAT

KIWI   Taran Noah Smith

MOLLY   June Havoc

SOLLY   June Havoc

WIKI   Taran Noah Smith

RAVEN

GRIP   Charles Dickens

MEMORY   Odin

THOUGHT   Odin

REINDEER

BLITZEN   Santa Claus

CUPID   Santa Claus

DANCER   Santa Claus

DONDER   Santa Claus

PRANCER   Santa Claus

RUDOLPH   Santa Claus

VIXEN   Santa Claus

ROOSTER

EARL   Elly May Clampett

SALAMANDER

SHADRACK
       Robert F. Kennedy

SEAL

DIANA
     William Randolph Hearst

Diana swam up to William Randolph Hearst's dock one day, and adopted him. Hearst dropped everything that he was doing and personally supervised the construction of a home for Diana. He built her a personal pen, and ensured that a plentiful supply of fish was available for her every day.

SIBERIAN TIGER

GREGORY	Tippi Hedren
LEIKA	Tippi Hedren
NIKKI	Tippi Hedren

SKUNK

PHEW	Vincent Price
SMELLY	Elly May Clampett

SNAKE

MISS EMILY SPINACH
Alice Roosevelt

The daughter of Teddy Roosevelt, she used to take her pet snake to official functions at the White House just to see what havoc she could create.

SQUIRREL

RICOTTE	Colette

TEDDY BEAR

WINNIE-THE-POOH
Christopher Robin

THRUSH

OLD BILL	Calvin Coolidge

TIGER

AMANI	Jack Paar

Jack Paar brought home a baby tiger, fed him from a bottle, and raised him at home. Still living in the house when he was full grown, Amani would fight Jack in the living room for the Sunday paper.

IVAN	Tippi Hedren
NATASHA	Tippi Hedren
SINGH SINGH	
	Tippi Hedren

TURKEY

JACK	Abraham Lincoln

TURTLE

CARL	Robin Williams

When he was a boy, Robin Williams wanted to set his pet turtle Carl free, so he flushed it down the toilet.

DINKY	Jonathan Brandis

VIETNAMESE POTBELLIED PIG

BETTY
Tiffani-Amber Thiessen

JERRY LEE	Luke Perry
VIOLET	Luke Perry

VULTURE

JURGATHA
Alexandre Dumas

Alexandre Dumas would walk his pet vulture Jurgatha down the Champs-Elysèes on a silver leash. The fancy French poodles on the walk were amazed by the many tricks that the vulture had been trained to do by Dumas.

WOLF

FREKI   Odin

Odin, the king of gods in Norse mythology, had his wolves Freki and Geri eat all of the meat served because he needed no food.

GERI   Odin

WORM

ALFRED   Susan Dey

Susan Dey was very devoted to her earthworm Alfred, feeding him on a diet of bread crumbs, fruit juice and cookies. Always fearful for his safety, she would deliver daily lectures to him on how he could avoid becoming dinner for some roving bird. Unfortunately, Susan felt that he was looking down, probably because he had been separated from his girlfriend, and she set him free.

CELEBRITY INDEX

ACHILLES

Balius	Horse
Xanthus	Horse

ACTAEON

Aello	Dog
Agre	Dog
Alce	Dog
Argus	Dog
Asbolus	Dog
Canache	Dog
Dromas	Dog
Hylactor	Dog
Labros	Dog
Lachne	Dog
Lebros	Dog
Lelaps	Dog
Leucite	Dog
Lycisa	Dog
Melampus	Dog
Melaneus	Dog
Pachytus	Dog
Poemenis	Dog
Stricte	Dog
Theron	Dog

AGAMEMNON

Aethe	Horse

ANN-MARGRET

Bubber	Cat
Melba	Cat
Sugar	Maltese

APOLLO

Aethon	Horse
Pegasus	Horse
Phlegon	Horse
Pyrois	Horse

ATHENA

Aethon	Horse

BARETTA

Fred	Cockatoo

BEN HUR

Aldebaran	Horse
Altair	Horse
Antares	Horse
Rigel	Horse

BIJAN

Bearface	Chow Chow
Charcoal	Chow Chow
Panda	Dog

BUDDHA

Kanthaka	Horse

BUDWEISER

Andy	Clydesdale
Baron	Clydesdale
Bill	Clydesdale
Buck	Clydesdale
Captain	Clydesdale
Commander	Clydesdale
Dean	Clydesdale
Duke	Clydesdale
Jake	Clydesdale
Mark	Clydesdale
Sammy	Clydesdale
Spuds Mackenzie	Bull Terrier

CALIGULA

Incitatus	Horse

CHARLEMAGNE

Blanchard	Horse
Tencendur	Horse

CHARO

Delilah	Chihuahua
Toro	Doberman Pinscher

CHATEAUBRIAND

Micetto	Cat

CHEOPS

Abakaru	Dog

CINDERELLA

Blank	Horse

MOHAMMED

Alborak	Horse
Al Kaswa	Camel
Fadda	Horse
Muezza	Cat

NAZIMOVA

Daisy	Wire Fox Terrier
Mike	Wire Fox Terrier

ODIN

Freki	Wolf
Geri	Wolf
Memory	Raven
Sleipner	Horse
Thought	Raven

ODYSSEUS

Argos	Dog

PANCHO

Loco	Horse

PHANTOM

Hero	Horse
Thunder	Horse

PINOCCHIO

Aladdin	Dog

PLUTO

Abaster	Horse
Abatos	Horse
Aeton	Horse
Alastor	Horse

POSEIDON

Sthenius	Horse

ROLAND

Veillantiff	Horse

SAKI

Gillie	Fox Terrier

SUPERGIRL

Comet	Horse

SUPERMAN

Krypto	Dog

TAMARLANE

Sharad-Nar-Al-Din	Horse

TARZAN

Cheetah	Chimpanzee

TERRY THOMAS

Archie	Dog

TIMUR

Sharad-Nar-Al-Din	Horse

TONTO

Paint	Horse
Scout	Horse
White Feller	Horse

XERXES

Strymon	Horse

ZORRO

Phantom	Horse
Tornado	Horse

WILLIE AAMES

Billy	Cat
Dreamer	Cat
Garfunkel	Iguana
Jigger	Persian
Shuttz	Doberman Pinscher
Simon	Iguana

KAREEM ABDUL-JABBAR

Bruno	Dog
Spencer	Rottweiler

EMILE ACHARD

Matapon	Cat

J. R. ACKERLEY

Tulip	Alsatian

ART ACORD

Black Beauty	Horse

BROOKE ADAMS

Scamper	Cat

DON ADAMS

Brandy	Miniature Poodle
Max	Miniature Poodle

Pleasure	Fox Hound	Philippe	Cat
Pride	Horse	Sam	Cat
Purple Star	Horse	Skipper	Cat

WALLIS ANNENBERG

Olivia — Shih Tzu

KING ARTHUR

Apollon	Dog

LITTLE ORPHAN ANNIE

Sandy — Dog

Bounce	Dog
Boy	Dog
Bran	Dog

CHRISTINA APPLEGATE

Kaanaloa — Cat

Bungey	Dog
Caball	Horse

ANNE ARCHER

Bordeaux	Dog
Boxey	Dog

Cavall	Dog
Clumsy	Dog
Colle	Dog

EVE ARDEN

Mollie Bee	Donkey
Orphan Annie	Lamb
Patches	Horse

Diamond	Dog
Gerland	Dog
Gerlert	Dog
Lamri	Horse
Lion	Dog

JANE ARDMORE

Keno — Russian Wolfhound

Luath	Dog
Luffra	Dog

LUCIE ARNAZ

Wickle — Dog

Orthrose	Dog
Phoebe	Dog

JAMES ARNESS

Matt	Bishon Frise
Miss Kitty	Bishon Frise

Spumador	Horse
Talbot	Dog
Toby	Dog
Trowneer	Dog

MATTHEW ARNOLD

Atossa	Persian
Blacky	Cat
Geist	Dachshund
Kaiser	Dog
Max	Dog
Toss	Persian

MARY KAY ASH

Gigi — Dog

ED ASNER

CoCo	Siamese
Miss Abigail	Cat
Mr. Essex	Cat
Pete	Parrot
Teddy Bear	Persian

PATRICIA ARQUETTE

Guntry — Cat

BEA ARTHUR

Charlie	German Shepherd
Jennifer	Doberman Pinscher
Ruby	Belgian Sheepdog

FRED ASTAIRE

Allison	Cockapoo
Early Bird	Horse
Gregory	Cockatiel
Over Anxious	Horse

JEAN ARTHUR

Fagin — Cat

Rainbow Tie Horse
Thumper Rabbit
Triplicate Horse

SEAN ASTIN
Byron Siberian Husky
Shelly Tabby

BROOKS ATKINSON
Cleo German Shepherd

RENE AUBERJONOIS
Jimmy Cat

W. H. AUDEN
Nerone Cat
Rhadame Cat

GENE AUTRY
Champion Horse
Dice Pinto Stallion
Lindy Horse
Pal Horse
Tony, Jr. Horse

LAUREN BACALL
Droopy Cocker Spaniel
Harvey Boxer
Puddle Cocker Spaniel

BARBARA BACH
Reno Cat

CATHERINE BACH
Ingo German Shepherd
Kitty Persian

BURT BACHARACH
Afternoon Delights Horse
Battle Royal Horse
Heartlight No. One Horse
Hoover Lhasa Apso
Le Solaret Horse
Noofy Newfoundland
Sole of the Matter Horse

DR. BORIS BAGDASSARROFF
Eashipur Balinese

JOEL BAILEY
Biscuit Cat

JIM BAKKER
Corky Yorkshire Terrier
Peaches Poodle

TAMMY FAYE BAKKER
Corky Yorkshire Terrier
Peaches Poodle

LUCILLE BALL
Ginger Belgian Schippenke
Junior German Shepherd
Tinker Toy Toy Poodle
Tinkerbell Poodle
Toy Fox Terrier
Whoopee Fox Terrier

KAYE BALLARD
Pockets Poodles
Punky Poodle
Shirley Poodle

ANNE BANCROFT
Marmalade Cat
Pongo Staffordshire Bull Terrier

TALLULAH BANKHEAD
Bonnie Mixed Breed
Cleo Mynah Bird
Daisy French Poodle
Dolly Siamese
Doloras Maltese Poodle
Flora Cat
Gaylord Bird
Hitchcock Sealyham Terrier
King Kong Monkey
Magnolia English Sheep Dog
Senegas Monkey
Winston Churchill Lion

Furball   Cat
FRED BERGENDORFF
Buster   Cat
INGMAR BERGMAN
Teddy   Poodle
INGRID BERGMAN
Ferdinando   Dachshund
SANDRA BERNHARD
CoCo   Dog
SARAH BERNHARDT
Bull   Dog
Fly   Dog
Hamlet   Dog
Miniccio   Dog
HALLE BERRY
Bumper   Maltese
Petey   Maltese
VALERIE BERTINELLI
George   Burmese
BILL BEYERS
Brie   Cat
Camembert   Cat
Gouda   Manx
Muenster   Cat
Velveeta   Cat
JACQUELINE BISSET
Fiddler   Cat
Monstrello   Cat
KAREN BLACK
Minnie   Labrador Retriever
LINDA BLAIR
Alice   Dog
Moogie   Terrier
Pilsner   Terrier
AMANDA BLAKE
Kemo   Lion
Little Clay   Cat

ROBERT BLAKE
Charlie Potatoes   Dog
BILL BLASS
Barnaby   Labrador Retriever
Brutus   Golden Retriever
Kate   Golden Retriever
Shelby   Golden Retriever
BETSY BLOOMINGDALE
Beverly   German Shepherd
Zozo   German Shepherd
DIRK BOGARDE
Bogie   Welsh Corgi
Candida   English Mastiff
Dobbin   Stallion
Rogan   Dog
Sinhue   Welsh Corgi
HUMPHREY BOGART
Dorarich Butch
              Sealyham Terrier
Droopy   Dog
Harvey   Boxer
Sluggy   Scottish Terrier
ERMA BOMBECK
Arlo   Irish Setter
Jessamyn   Poodle
NAPOLEON BONAPARTE
Ali   Horse
Austerlitz   Horse
Coco   Horse
Desiree   Arabian
Jaffa   Horse
Marengo   Horse
Marie   Horse
Pumpernickel   Horse
Roitelet   Horse
Tauris   Arabian
Vizir   Horse
Wagram   Horse

❖

Bobby Socks	Shih Tzu
Clark	Cat

GEORGE BRENT

Whiskey	Pug

BOBBIE BRESEE

Champagne	Cat

MORGAN BRITTANY

Roxie	Dog

CUBBY BROCCOLI

Don't Stop The Music	Horse

CHARLES BRONSON

Cassie	Dog
Dennis	Horse
K-Doc	Horse
Psyche	Horse
Robbie	Horse

ANNE BRONTE

Flossy	Spaniel

CHARLOTTE BRONTE

Tiger	Cat

EMILY BRONTE

Keeper	Bull Mastiff

MEL BROOKS

Marmalade	Cat
Pongo	Staffordshire Bull Terrier

BUSTER BROWN

Tige	Dog

CHARLIE BROWN

Snoopy	Beagle

HELEN GURLEY BROWN

Samantha	Siamese

JOHNNY MACK BROWN

Rebel	Horse

TOM BROWN

Bonso	Dog

VELVET BROWN

Angelina	Horse
Blaze King	Horse
Fancy	Horse
George	Horse
Miss Ada	Horse
Mrs. James	Horse
Sir Pericles	Horse
The Pie	Horse

ELIZABETH BARRETT BROWNING

Faunus	Dog
Flush	Cocker Spaniel

ROBERT BROWNING

Flush	Cocker Spaniel

KING ROBERT THE BRUCE

Help and Hand	Scottish Deerhound

ZACHARY TY BRYAN

Sauki	Shih Tzu
Snowball	Rabbit

JAMES BUCHANAN

Lara	Newfoundland

WILLIAM F. BUCKLEY, JR.

Fred	King Charles Spaniel
Lowey	King Charles Spaniel

TARA BUCKMAN

Ashley	Cat

JOHN BUECHLER

Cinema	Cocker Spaniel

DAGWOOD BUMSTEAD

Daisy	Dog

PAUL BUNYAN

Babe	Ox
Nero	Dog
Skookun	Dog
Zip	Terrier

SID CAESAR

Cindy	Dog
Conus	Rottweiler
Julius	Great Dane
Sascha	Siberian Husky

DEAN CAIN

Mocha	Weimaraner

JAMES M. CAIN

Nickie	Cat

K CALLAN

Momcat	Cat
P2	Mongrel
Paws	Cat
Sweden	Mongrel

MICHAEL CALLAN

Momcat	Cat
Paws	Cat

MARIA CALLAS

Djedda	Poodle
Pixie	Poodle
Toy	Poodle

GLEN CAMPBELL

Boone	Dog

JULIA CAMPBELL

Bianca	Cat
Caliban	Dog

TISHA CAMPBELL

Sojah	Chow Chow

LOUIS J. CAMUTI

Baron	Dachshund

JIMMY CANNON

Jupiter	Sheepdog

KAREL CAPEK

Percy	Cat
Philip	Cat
Pudlenka	Cat
Rogue	Cat
Scamp	Cat

TRUMAN CAPOTE

Cinnamon	Dog

JENNIFER CAPRIATI

Bianca	Dog

ROGER A. CARAS

Bozo	Boston Terrier
Clothild the User	Cat
Eartha Cat	Cat
Maridadi	Cat
Michael	Cat
Siafu	Cat
Sumfun Abigail	Siamese
Tom	Cat

LORD CARDIGAN

Ronald	Horse

MARIAH CAREY

Baby	Horse
Ninja	Persian
Thompkins	Persian

THOMAS CARLYLE

Columbine	Cat

JUDY CARNE

Clyde	Dog

DAVID CARRADINE

Indian Woman	Horse

LEO CARRILLO

Conquistador	Horse

GUY WETMORE CARRYL

Zut	Cat

JOANNE CARSON

Bucephalus	Doberman Pinscher
China	Dog
Cinnamon	Dog
Muffin	Yorkshire Terrier
Pooh Bear	Dog
Samantha	Yorkshire Terrier

JOHNNY CARSON
Muffin   Yorkshire Terrier
Samantha   Yorkshire Terrier

KIT CARSON
Apache   Horse

SUNSET CARSON
Silver   Horse

AMY CARTER
Grits   Mixed Breed
Misty Malarky Ying Yang   Cat

JIMMY CARTER
Bozo   Dog
Lady Lee   Horse

GABRIELLE CARTERIS
Calvin Peoples   Cat

BARBARA CARTLAND
Duke   Labrador Retriever

ADAM CARTWRIGHT
Beauty   Horse

BEN CARTWRIGHT
Buck   Horse

HOSS CARTWRIGHT
Chub   Horse

LITTLE JOE CARTWRIGHT
Cochise   Horse

DAVID CASSIDY
Cassy   Dog
Dainty   Dog
Happy   Dog
Johnny's Image   Horse
Pepper   Dog
Smilin' Sam   Dog
Tiger   Dog

HOPALONG CASSIDY
Topper   Horse

JACK CASSIDY
Smokey   Cat

CATHERINE THE GREAT
Tom Anderson
          English Whippet

MARY JO CATLETT
Sonny   Cat

GEORGE CATLIN
Charley   Horse

KIM CATTRALL
Nellie Bly   Siamese
Salem   Cat

WILT CHAMBERLAIN
Zap   Cat
Zip   Cat

RAYMOND CHANDLER
Taki   Persian

CHARLIE CHAPLIN
Boots   Dog
Teddy   Dog

NICK CHARLES
Asta   Wire Fox Terrier

KING CHARLES II
Old Rowley   Horse

KING CHARLES IX
Caron   Water Spaniel
Comte   Water Spaniel
Liline   English Toy Spaniel

KING CHARLES VIII
Savoy   Horse

PRINCE CHARLES
Bandit   Pony
Harvey   Labrador Retriever
Honey   Welsh Corgi
Poor Pooh
       Jack Russell Terrier
San Quinina   Polo Pony
Sombra   Polo Pony
Tigger   Jack Russell Terrier

LESLIE CHARLESON
Freeway — Cocker Spaniel

CHEF SAAD CHAZI
Shiva — Cat

AGATHA CHRISTIE
Bingo — Terrier
James — Dog
Peter — Wire Fox Terrier
Treacle — Manchester Terrier

WILLIAM CHRISTOPHER
Pepper — Beagle

JOHN SPENCER CHURCHILL
Lady Arabella — Cat
Princess Sophie Louise — Cat

WINSTON CHURCHILL
Arab — Horse
Blackie — Cat
Margate — Cat
Mr. Punch — Dog
Nelson — Cat
Rufus — Poodle
Tango — Cat
Traveller — Horse

EL CID
Babieca — Horse
The Dolt — Horse

CISCO KID
Diablo — Horse

ELLY MAY CLAMPETT
Cousin Bess — Chimpanzee
Duke — Bloodhound
Earl — Rooster
Fairchild — Bear
Homer — Pigeon
Racky — Raccoon
Rusty — Cat
Skippy — Dog
Smelly — Skunk

DICK CLARK
Alice — Dog
Bernardo — Dog
Gypsy — Cat
Lucille — Dalmatian
Maybelline — Dog
Molly — Weimaraner

DWIGHT CLARK
Crystal — Chow Chow
Johnson — Chow Chow

SUSAN CLARK
Joey — Shih Tzu
Lazlo — Dog

SANTA CLAUS
Blitzen — Reindeer
Cupid — Reindeer
Dancer — Reindeer
Donder — Reindeer
Prancer — Reindeer
Rudolph — Reindeer
Vixen — Reindeer

PRESIDENT BILL CLINTON
Socks — Cat

GEORGE CLOONEY
Max — Pig

GLENN CLOSE
Gaby — Coton de Tulear

BUFFALO BILL CODY
Billy — Horse
Brigham — Horse
Buckskin Joe — Horse
Gray Ghost — Horse
Isham — Horse
King — Horse
McKinley — Horse
Muson — Horse
Old Charlie — Horse
Old Smoky — Horse

Tuck Canary

ALICE COOPER

Angel Boa Constrictor

GARY COOPER

Flash Horse
Zora Afghan Hound

MIRIAM COOPER

Mike Dog
Pat Dog
Pierre Poodle

DAVID COPPERFIELD

Dickens Cat

KATHERINE CORNELL

Fluff Dog

HERNANDO CORTEZ

El Morzillo Horse

BILL COSBY

Black Watch Moonstruck
Dog

VICTOR COSTA

D'or King Charles Spaniel

LOU COSTELLO

Bazooka Horse
Blue Baby Horse
Bold Bazooka Horse
Chico Dog
Laddie Dog
Lassie Dog
Lolly C. Horse

KEVIN COSTNER

Rosalita Labrador Retriever

BRISCOE COUNTY, JR.

Comet Horse

KATIE COURIC

Frank Cat

WILLIAM COWPER

Beau Spaniel

ED COX

Rocket Labrador Retriever

BUSTER CRABBE

Falcon Horse

ICHABOD CRANE

Gunpowder Horse

STEPHEN CRANE

Flannel Dog
Powder Puff Dog
Ruby Dog

WES CRAVEN

Bruno Cat
Grip Dog
Hillary Cat

CHRISTINA CRAWFORD

Daisy Dog
Pappy Horse
Pepper Dog

JOAN CRAWFORD

Beauty Horse
Cliquot French Poodle

JOHNNY CRAWFORD

Two Bits Horse

RICHARD CRENNA

Luci Persian

DOUG CRISTY

Rasta Pit Bull

JOHN CROMWELL

Gobo Polo Pony

A. J. CRONIN

Blix Airedale Terrier
Bunker Sealyham Terrier
Sally Cocker Spaniel
Sandy Cairn Terrier

WALTER CRONKITE

Dancer Cat

BING CROSBY

Broadway Joe Horse
Ligaroti Horse

Zombie	Horse

GARY CROSBY

Red Dog	Poodle

MARY FRANCES CROSBY

Emmine	Horse
Romeo	Alley Cat

TOM CRUISE

Joseph	Labrador Retriever

BILLY CRYSTAL

Mittons	Cat

GEORGE CUKOR

Amanda	Dachshund
Sasha	Standard Poodle
Solo	Dachshund

QUINN CUMMINGS

Ginger	Dog
Pooh	Calico

GEORGE ARMSTRONG CUSTER

Blucher	Dog
Byron	Dog
Cardigan	Dog
Commanche	Horse
Custis Lee	Horse
Dandy	Horse
Don Juan	Horse
Ginnie	Pointer
Harry	Horse
Jack Rucker	Horse
Maida	Dog
Phil Sheridan	Horse
Roanoke	Horse
Vic	Horse

EMMET DALTON

Katie	Horse
Red Buck	Horse

VIDA DANA

Puff	Dog

BEVERLY D'ANGELO

Evalita	Dog

JOHN D'AQUISTO

Bruiser	Shih Tzu
Buddy	Dog

WENDY DARLING

Nana	Newfoundland

LINDA DARNELL

Spot	Dog

ERASMUS DARWIN

Persian Snow	Cat

ROBERT DAVENPORT

Jet	Dog
Rocky	Cat

BETTE DAVIS

Boojum	Dog
Meg	Scottish Terrier
Schatzie	Dog

JEFFERSON DAVIS

Kentucky	Horse
Tartar	Horse

SAMMY DAVIS, JR.

Bojangles	Toy Poodle
Columbus	Toy Poodle
Dinky	Toy Poodle
Dr. Sam	Toy Poodle

PAM DAWBER

Red	Australian Cattle Dog

DORIS DAY

Autie Murphy	Dog
Autumn	Dog
Barney Miller	Dog
Biggest	Dog
Bobo	Dog
Bubbles	Poodle
Bucky	Dog
Charlie	Poodle
Chipper	Dog
Daisy	Collie

❖

Daisy-June	Dog
Dillon	Dog
El Tigre	Dog
Heineken	Dog
Honey	Dog
Joey	Bird
Miss Lucy	Cat
Mr. Lucky	Cat
Muffy	Poodle
Rudy	Dachshund
Schatzie	Dachshund
Sneakers	Cat
Snowy	Dog
Tiger	Poodle
Tiny	Dog
Trixie	Dog
Varmit	Dog

FRANCES DAY

Bill	Bulldog

LARAINE DAY

Igor	Bull Mastiff

EDDIE DEAN

Copper	Palomino
Flash	Horse
White Cloud	Horse

JAMES DEAN

Louis XIV	Cat
Marcus	Siamese
Strudel	Dachshund
Tuck	Dog

EDWARD J.DEBARTOLO, JR.

Cleo	Great Dane

YVONNE DE CARLO

Little King	Horse
Pepe	German Shepherd

CHARLES DE GAULLE

Gris-Gris	Cat

GLORIA DEHAVEN

Curtis	Cat
Daisy	Cat
Leo	Cat

OLIVIA DE HAVILLAND

Bouboule	Bulldog

ROBERT DELAUNAY

Anthony	Cat

DOM DELUISE

Goo Goo	Cat
Midnight	Cockapoo
Nancy	Cockapoo
Sharky	Cat
Tiffany	Cat

CECIL B. DEMILLE

Major Homer Q. Putnam	Dog

WILLIAM DEMILLE

Major Homer Q. Putnam	Dog

TOMIE DE PAOLA

Bingley	Airedale Terrier
Foshay	Abyssinian
Madison	Welsh Terrier

BO DEREK

Aiwa	German Shepherd
Amber	Greyhound
Angel	Andalusian
Angus	Parrot
Bolero	Greyhound
Buttercup	Palomino
Carita	Andalusian
Celosa	Andalusian
Centauro	Andalusian
China	Greyhound
Cif	German Shepherd
Coon Dog	Maine Coon
Corason	Paint/Andalusian

❖

| Preppy | Mastiff |
| Scruffy | Mixed Breed |

CHARLES DICKENS

Grip	Raven
Mrs. Bouncer	Pomeranian
Snittle Timbery	Dog
Sultan	Irish Bloodhound
Timber Doodle	Dog
Tumber	Dog
Turk	Mastiff
Wilhelmina	Cat

EMILY DICKINSON

| Carlo | Dog |

DIGBY DIEHL

| Angel | Dog |

MARLENE DIETRICH

| King John | Horse |

BARRY DILLER

| Whip | Labrador Retriever |

PHYLLIS DILLER

| Phearless | Lhasa Apso |

MARSHAL MATT DILLON

| Buck | Horse |

ISAK DINESEN

Duck	Scottish Deerhound
Osceola	Dog
Pasop	Alsatian
Pepper	Dandie Dinmont

WALT DISNEY

| Duchess | Poodle |
| Sunnee | Chow Chow |

SHANNEN DOHERTY

Bismark	Rottweiler
Clancy Muldoon	
	Golden Retriever
Elfie	German Shepherd
Julio	Dove
Old Dominion	Horse

Palomo	Dove
Pissaro	Dove
Precious Penelope	
	Labrador Retriever
Silly Sally	Golden Retriever

SENATOR BOB DOLE

| Leader | |
| | Miniature Schnauzer |

ELINOR DONAHUE

| Mary Elizabeth | |
| | Scottish Terrier |

PHIL DONAHUE

| Tida | Maltese |

ROBERT DONNER

Groucho	Cat
Noodle	Cat
Sophie	Cat
Zelda	Cat

STEPHEN DORFF

Clarence	Cat
Lincoln	Airedale Terrier
Patches	Cat
Tigger	Cat

DUDLEY DO-RIGHT

| Steed | Horse |

HENRY DOUGLAS

| Ashby | Horse |

KIRK DOUGLAS

Sparkle	
	King Charles Spaniel
Teddy	Poodle

MIKE DOUGLAS

Duke	Great Dane
Love	German Shepherd
Lucy	Silky Terrier

TONY DOW

| Bumpy | Otter |
| Magnolia | Bearded Collie |

DWIGHT D. EISENHOWER

Caacie	Dog
Heidi	Weimaraner
Spunky	Scottish Terrier
Telek	Scottish Terrier

ROBIN EISENMAN

Boris	Cat
Bubie	Siamese
Ferd	Cat
Natasha	Russian Blue

CHUCK EISENMANN

Hobo	German Shepherd
London	German Shepherd
Raura	German Shepherd
Venus	German Shepherd

T. S. ELIOT

Admetus	Cat
Asparagus	Cat
Bustopher Jones	Cat
Demeter	Cat
Electra	Cat
George Pushdragon	Cat
Great Rumpuscat	Cat
Grizabella	Cat
Growltiger	Cat
Gumbie	Cat
Gus	Cat
Jellicle Cat	Cat
Jellylorum	Cat
Jennyanydots	Cat
Lady Griddlebone	Cat
Macavity	Cat
Mr. Mistoffolees	Cat
Mungojerrie	Cat
Munkustrap	Cat
Old Deuteronomy	Cat
Pettipaws	Cat
Quaxo	Cat
Rum Tum Tugger	Cat
Rumpleteazer	Cat
Skimbleshanks	Cat
Tumblebrutus	Cat
Wiscus	Cat

QUEEN ELIZABETH I

Aureole	Horse
Tilbury	Horse

QUEEN ELIZABETH II

Above Suspicion	Horse
Alexander	Horse
Bellboy	Horse
Betsy	Horse
Burmese	Horse
Bussaco	Stallion
Centennial	Horse
Columbus	Horse
Cossack	Horse
Dookie	Welsh Corgi
Doutelle	Horse
High Veldt	Horse
Honey	Welsh Corgi
Imperial	Horse
Jane	Welsh Corgi
Johnny	Sealyham Terrier
Sue	Welsh Corgi
Sugar	Welsh Corgi
Sultan	Horse
Winston	Horse

GORDON "WILD BILL" ELLIOT

Stormy	Horse

BILL ELLIOTT

Sonny	Horse

PATRICIA ELLIS

Major	German Shepherd

KELLY EMBERG

Bobby	Rabbit
Gus	Dog
Snuffy	Dog

Boo-Dyes — Siamese
Brownie — Rottweiler
Coco — Rottweiler
Cookie — Rottweiler
Dos — Australian Cattle Dog
Kitty — Dog
Pappillon — Dog
Zeus — Rottweiler

GRACIE FIELDS
Sandy — Dog

TOTIE FIELDS
Bubbles — Dog

ALBERT FINNEY
So She Sleeps — Horse

CARRIE FISHER
Buddy — Dog
Sweetie — Rottweiler

F. SCOTT FITZGERALD
Bouillabaisse — Mixed Breed
Chopin — Persian
Ezra Pound — Mixed Breed
Jerry — Mixed Breed
Muddy Water — Mixed Breed
Trouble — Bloodhound

ZELDA FITZGERALD
Bouillabaisse — Mixed Breed
Chopin — Persian
Ezra Pound — Mixed Breed
Jerry — Mixed Breed
Muddy Water — Mixed Breed
Trouble — Bloodhound

ROBERTA FLACK
Caruso — Siamese

FANNIE FLAGG
Bruce — Persian
Mister Roots — Cat
Tallulah — Cat

RHONDA FLEMING
Sparkey — Dog

RICHARD FLORIO
Baby Jane — Yorkshire Terrier

ERROL FLYNN
Arno — Schnauzer
Bes Mudi — Siamese
Chico — Monkey
Man Friday — Dog

JOAN FONTAINE
Calico — Persian
Carnoustie — West Highland Terrier
Fang — German Shepherd
Hazber — Poodle

EILEEN FORD
Kiki — Alley Cat

GERALD FORD
Chan — Cat
Jackie — Golden Retriever
Liberty — Golden Retriever
Misty — Golden Retriever
Shan — Siamese

GLENN FORD
Betty — Chicken

WALLY FORD
Dick — Great Dane

MILOS FORMAN
Matej — Dog
Rek — Dog

NATHAN BEDFORD FORREST
King Phillip — Horse

JOHN FORSYTHE
Fallon — Toy Poodle
Krystle — Toy Poodle
Mamselle Bebette — Horse
Targa — Horse

☙ CELEBRITY INDEX

Sid Dog

SERGE GAINSBOURG

Nana Bull Terrier

DOROTHY GALE

Toto Cairn Terrier

GINA GALLEGO

Biscuit Cat
MacBarker Dalmatian

PAUL GALLICO

Chilla Cat
Chin Cat
Limpy Cat
Lulu II Siamese
Morris Cat
Pitipoo Siamese
Tante Hedwig Cat
Tough Charlie Cat
Tough Tom Cat
Wuzzy Cat

DON GALLOWAY

Whiskey Dog

JOHN GALSWORTHY

Chris Spaniel

GRETA GARBO

Polly Parrot

AVA GARDNER

Lucky Dog
Morgan Dog

JOHN GARDNER

George Yorkshire Terrier
Smudge Cat

JAMES A. GARFIELD

Kit Horse
Veto Dog

JUDY GARLAND

Chou Chou Poodle
Eddie Collie

JAMES GARNER

Nikki Mixed Breed

LEIF GARRETT

Nadia Dog

GREER GARSON

Ack Ack Horse
Gogo Dog
Ramaahipati IV Siamese

JENNIE GARTH

Golden Boy Jet Horse
Roadie Cat
Sasha Toy Poodle
Zack Toy Poodle

THEOPHILE GAUTIER

Enjolras Cat
Gavroche Cat
Madame Theophile Cat
Zizi Cat
Zobeide Cat
Zuleika Cat
Zulema Cat

JOHN GAVIN

Julie Bishon Frise

JOHN GAY

Shock Dog

MARGARET COOPER GAY

Picklepuss Cat

JANET GAYNOR

Missy Dog
Super Cat Cat

TONY GEARY

Taylor Persian

DAVID LLOYD GEORGE

Bang Chow Chow
Beauty Chow Chow
Bismark Mixed Breed
Chong Chow Chow
Dai Pembrokeshire Corgi
Diveidi Dog

GEORGE GOBEL

Bosco	Cat

ARTHUR GODFREY

Alyfar	Arabian Stallion
Goldie	Horse

BOB GOEN

Johnson	Golden Retriever

GARY DAVID GOLDBERG

Ubu	Hound

BARRY GOLDWATER

Cyclone	Dog
Sunny	Mule

VALERIA GOLINO

Bebop	Cat

DR. JANE GOODALL

Fifi	Chimpanzee
Gigi	French Poodle
Goblin	Chimpanzee

DEBORAH GOODRICH

Louis	Siamese
Nicky	Cat

MARIANNE GORDON

Caboodle	Cat
Kit	Cat

RUTH GORDON

Sacha	Poodle

BERRY GORDY

Powis Castle	Horse

LESLEY GORE

Agatha	Cocker Spaniel

EDWARD GOREY

Amy	Cat
Billy	Cat
Charlie	Cat
George	Cat
Goerge	Cat
Sukie	Cat
Weedon	Cat

EYDIE GORME

Casey	Dog
Nugget	Dog
Roxy	Dog
Sonny	Dog

ROBERT GOULET

Lance	German Shepherd

BETTY GRABLE

Big Noise	Horse
Punky	Poodle

STEFFI GRAF

Ben	Boxer
Max	German Shepherd
Zar	German Shepherd

BILLY GRAHAM

Belshazzar	Great Pyrenees

STEWART GRANGER

Me-Too	Tibetan Spaniel

CARY GRANT

Suzie	Poodle

ULYSSES SIMPSON GRANT

Billy Button	Shetland Pony
Butcher Boy	Horse
Cincinnatus	Horse
Egypt	Horse
Faithful	Newfoundland
Fox	Horse
Ismael	Horse
Jack	Horse
Jeff Davis	Horse
Jennie	Horse
Julia	Horse
Kangaroo	Horse
Leopard	Arabian Stallion
Linden Tree	Arabian Stallion
Mary	Horse
Maud S.	Horse
Reb	Shetland Pony

St. Louis | Horse
LINDA GRAY
Giorgio | German Shepherd
Michael Moo | Sheep Dog
Orange Oliver | Cat
MICHAEL GRAY
Butch | Poodle
Buzzy | Wire Fox Terrier
Felix | Chicken
Figaro | Parakeet
George | Poodle
Maggie | Poodle
Melancholy | Cat
Peppy | Wire Fox Terrier
KATHRYN GRAYSON
Didi | Dog
Kiki | Dog
Meeny | Dog
Moose | Dog
Panda | Dog
Rumples | Dog
Scruffy | Dog
BRIAN AUSTIN GREEN
Bo | Boa Constrictor
Cube | Rottweiler
LORNE GREENE
Ginger | Dog
King | Dog
SIR WILFRED GRENFEL
Brin | Sled Dog
WAYNE GRETZKY
Glen Kate | Horse
Sun Brandy | Horse
JOEL GREY
Betti | Cat
MERV GRIFFIN
Patrick | Irish Setter
Poochie | Irish Setter

Puddy | Persian
MELANIE GRIFFITH
Casey | Lion
Neil | Lion
Partner | Lion
TAMMY GRIMES
Bedford | Cat
Teegy | Cat
The Peach | Cat
DAVID GROH
Dukey | Cat
Fluff | Himalayan
CORNELIA GUEST
Lyle | West Highland Terrier
PEGGY GUGGENHEIM
Borotra | Sealyham Terrier
Emily | Lhasa Apso
Giorgio | Persian
Gypsy | Persian
Kachina
| Tibetan Lhasa Terrier
Robin | Sealyham Terrier
Romeo | Cat
Sans Lendemain | Persian
White Angel | Lhasa Apso
TEXAS GUINAN
Snowflake | Horse
ALEC GUINNESS
Percy | Parrot
DEVON GUMMERSALL
Black & White | Cat
Nick | German Shepherd
AMES GUNN
Kliban | Siamese
Mo | Maine Coon
SIR GUYON
Brigliadore | Horse

MERLE HAGGARD
Pepper	Toy Terrier
Wawe	Toy Terrier

FESTUS HAGGEN
Ruth	Mule

H. R. HALDEMAN
Amy	Dog
Dottie	Dog

MONTE HALL
Pardner	Horse

ALEX HALEY
Buttons	Yorkshire Terrier

DEIDRE HALL
Kashka	Cat
Max	Labrador Retriever
Molly	Golden Retriever

GEORGE HAMILTON
Mitzi	Yorkshire Terrier

HARRY HAMLIN
Meno	Cat

GENERAL WADE HAMPTON
Beauregard	Horse
Butler	Horse

JAMES HAMPTON
Gucci	Chow Chow

LARRY HANKIN
Butch	Fish
Dime	Fish
Frog	Fish
Horizon	Cat
Nickle	Fish
Penny	Fish
The Wonder Fish	Fish

WARREN G. HARDING
Caswell Laddie Boy	Airedale Terrier
Hub	Boston Terrier
Laddie Boy	Airedale Terrier
Oh Boy	Bulldog

THOMAS HARDY
Kiddleywinkempoops	Cat
Moss	Dog
Snowdove	Cat
Trot	Cat
Wessex	Wire Fox Terrier

JEAN HARLOW
Oscar	Dog

MARK HARMON
Cooper	Australian Cattle Dog
Frank	Australian Cattle Dog
Paddy	Australian Cattle Dog
Red	Australian Cattle Dog
Ryan	Collie
Steve	Cat

VALERIE HARPER
Archie	Dog
Billy the Kid	Dog
Jessie	Dog

BILL HARRIS
Diamond	Labrador Retriever
Kitty Carlisle	Abyssinian

JULIE HARRIS
Teresa	Yorkshire Terrier

ROSE HARRIS
Spike	Cat

BENJAMIN HARRISON
Abdullah	Horse
Billy	Horse
Dash	Red Setter
John	Horse
Lexington	Horse
Mr. Protection	Possum
Mr. Reciprocity	Possum
Old Whiskers	Goat

JENILEE HARRISON

| Amber | Dog |
| April | Dog |

REX HARRISON

Bedford	Alley Cat
Homer	Basset Hound
Jason	Basset Hound
Phantom	Boxer
Tara	Basset Hound
William	Sealyham Terrier

WILLIAM HENRY HARRISON

| His Wiskers | Goat |
| Sukey | Cow |

MARY HART

| Pumpkin | |
| | King Charles Spaniel |

WILLIAM S. HART

| Cactus Kate | Horse |
| Fritz | Horse |

MARIETTE HARTLEY

Bilbo	Cat
Cujo	Dog
Daisy	Golden Retriever

LISA HARTMAN

| Bear | Persian |

CYNTHIA HARVEY

| Tabitha | Maine Coon |

DAVID HASSELHOFF

Charlie	Parrot
Jenny	Pomeranian
Killer	Pomeranian
Kitty Kat	Cat
Rusty	Shih Tzu
Silky	Terrier
Sissy	Toy Dachshund
Toto	Cairn Terrier
Weiner	
	Miniature Dachshund

RICHARD HATCH

| Lee Chan | Cat |

DENYS FINCH HATTON

| Sirius | Dog |

JUNE HAVOC

Bootsie	Poodle
Daisy	Guinea Pig
Jimmy	Guinea Pig
Molly	Rat
Mumshay	Spaniel
Samba	Guinea Pig
Sambo	Guinea Pig
Solly	Rat

TOM HAYDEN

| Scott | Border Collie |
| Taxi | Labrador Retriever |

GABBY HAYES

| Calico | Horse |

HELEN HAYES

Camille	Dog
Charro	Poodle
Chiquita	Poodle
Hoopla	Dog

RUTHERFORD B. HAYES

| Grim | Dog |
| Miss Pussy | Cat |

JORIS-KARL HAYSMANS

| Mouche | Cat |

RITA HAYWORTH

Knockwurst	Dachshund
Lilac	Dachshund
Mink	Dachshund
Pookles	Dog

EDITH HEAD

| Gainsborough | Russian Blue |

CHICK HEARN

| Ashley | Bichon Frise |
| Oliver | Bichon Frise |

LAFCADIO HEARN

Tama	Cat

PATTY HEARST

Arrow	Dog

WILLIAM RANDOLPH HEARST

Diana	Seal
Helen	Dachshund

TIPPI HENDREN

Alice	Lion
Bacchus	Lion
Berries	Lion
Billy	Lion
Boomer	Lion
Bridget	Lion
Brutus	Lion
Buster	Leopard
Casey	Lion
Cheeries	Lion
Chelsea	Lion
Cindi	Lion
Cleopatra	Leopard
Debbie	Lion
Frankie	Lion
Gilligan	Lion
Gregory	Siberian Tiger
Igor	Lion
Ike	Lion
Ivan	Tiger
Jenny	Lion
Johnny	Lion
Katrina	Lion
Kura	Elephant
Leika	Siberian Tiger
Lena	Lion
Lillian	Lion
Lurch	Lion
Mariah	Leopard
Melanie	Lion
Merrie	Lion
Mike	Lion
Nancy	Lion
Natasha	Tiger
Needra	Lion
Neil	Lion
Nero	Lion
Nikki	Siberian Tiger
Noelle	Lion
Partner	Lion
Penny	Lion
Pepper	Leopard
Pharaoh	Cheetah
Rhett Butler	Cheetah
Robbie, Jr.	Lion
Scarface	Lion
Scarlett O'Hara	Cheetah
Shelia	Lion
Singh Singh	Tiger
Timbo	Elephant
Togar	Lion
Tongaru	Lion
Trans	Lion
Zazu	Bengal Tiger
Zuru	Lion

ROBERT A. HEINLEIN

Pixel	Cat

CHUCK HEMINGWAY

Maxfield Blue	Cat
Patches	Cat

ERNEST HEMINGWAY

Alley Cat	Cat
Blackie	Springer Spaniel
Boise	Cat
Cuba	Cat
Mr. Feather Puss	Cat
Pilar	Cat
Princess	Cat
Skunk	Cat
Whitehead	Cat

Katie	Dog
Lady	Dog
Maggie	Dog
Mannie	Dog
Maybell	Cat
Mister	Cat
Monroe	Cat
Napoleon	Goat
Phoebe	Cat
Pinto	Dog
Poacher	Dog
Puppy	Dog
Randy	Dog
Sam	Dog
Sargeant	Dog
Shadow	Dog
Smoke	Dog
Tatters	Dog
Tom	Cat
Walter	Pigeon

DAVID HOLT

Skeeper	Dog

TIM HOLT

Casey	Dog
Duke	Horse
Lightning	Horse

THOMAS HOOD

Dash	Dog
Pepperpot	Cat
Scratchaway	Cat
Sootikins	Cat
Tabitha Longclaws	Cat

GENERAL JOSEPH HOOKER

Lookout	Horse

HERBERT HOOVER

Big Ben	Fox Terrier
Eaglehurst Gillette	Irish Setter
Glen	Scotch Collie
King Tut	German Shepherd
Pat	German Shepherd
Patrick	Irish Wolfhound
Sonnie	Fox Terrier
Weejie	Norwegian Elkhound
Yukon	Malamute

J. EDGAR HOOVER

Cindy	Cairn Terrier
G. Boy	Cairn Terrier

BOB HOPE

Bob	Cat
CoCo	Lhasa Apso
Gilby	Maltese
Mike	Poodle
Recession	Basset Hound
Snow Job	Alsatian

BO HOPKINS

Bogie	Labrador Retriever
Candy	Golden Retriever

ROGER HORCHOW

Kittens	Cat
Valentine	Labrador Retriever

JOHN HOUSEMAN

Caroline	Dachshund
Jasper	Dachshund
Virgil Thomson	Dachshund

SAM HOUSTON

Bruin	Horse
Jack	Horse
Old Pete	Stallion

WHITNEY HOUSTON

Marilyn	Cat
Miste	Cat
Misteblu	Persian

JEAN HOWARD

Brutus	Dog
Found	Maltese

‥

Gypsy	Elephant
Jabbar	Giraffe
Lola	Llama
Louis	Llama
Max	Chimpanzee
Mr. Tibbs	Ram
Muscles	Boa Constrictor
Prince	Deer
Princess	Deer
Simba	Lion
Spring	Peacock
Winter	Peacock

GENERAL STONEWALL JACKSON

Old Sorrel	Horse

VICTORIA JACKSON

Angel	Cat
Jolson	Cat

MARC JACOBS

Tiger	Dalmatian

BRUCE JAMES

Bertha Lou	Labrador Retriever

CHARLES JAMES

Sputnik	Beagle

FRANK JAMES

Dan	Horse

JESSE JAMES

Cyrock	Horse
Katie	Horse
Red Fox	Horse
Siroc	Horse

JOHN JAMES

Camille	Rhodesian Ridgeback
Cub	Border Collie

P. D. JAMES

Cuthbert	Cat
Pansy	Cat

DICK & JANE

Puff	Cat
Spot	Dog

WRANGLER JANE

Pecos	Horse

THOMAS JEFFERSON

Bremo	Horse
Dick	Mockingbird
Diomede	Horse
Eagle	Horse
Tecumseh	Horse
Wellington	Horse

LUCKY JENKINS

Banjo	Horse

WAYLON JENNINGS

Tinker Bell	Cat

ELROY JETSON

Astro	Dog

ARTE JOHNSON

Kleine	Cocker Spaniel
Knudle	Cocker Spaniel

DR. SAMUEL JOHNSON

Hodge	Cat
Lilly	Cat

JAY JOHNSON

Renfield	Cat

KAY JOHNSON

Figero	Doberman Pinscher

LUCI JOHNSON

Astronaut	Dog
Boris	Hamster
Pecosa	Beagle

LYNDON JOHNSON

Beagle	Beagle
Blanco	Collie
Chinkapen	Dog
Dumpling	Beagle
Edgar	Beagle
Freckles	Beagle

Her	Beagle
Him	Beagle
J. Edgar	Beagle
Kim	Beagle
Little Beagle	Beagle
Little Chap	Beagle
Rover	Dog
Yuki	Mixed Breed

GENERAL ALBERT JOHNSTON

Fire-Eater	Horse
Fannie	Horse

BUCK JONES

Silver	Horse
White Eagle	Horse

JACK JONES

Jonesey	Dog
PeeDee	Dog

QUINCY JONES

Lucy	Cat

SHIRLEY JONES

Chrissie	Dog
Cyrano	Dog
Lu-Lu	Shih Tzu
Millie	Persian
Rebel	Cat
Samantha	Cat
Skoshie	Poodle
Smokey	Cat

DOROTHY JORDAN

Buck	Dog

EARLE JORGENSEN

Acero	German Shepherd
Heidi	German Shepherd
Poochie	German Shepherd

CHIEF JOSEPH

Ebenezer	Horse

JACKIE JOSEPH

Baby Mew	Cat

Purcy	Cat
The Mooter	Dog

MICHAEL JOSEPH

Charles O'Malley	Siamese
Mina Mina Joseph	Cat

MILLA JOVOVICH

Doc	Chihuahua

JAMES JOYCE

Sans Lendemain	Persian

ROSEMARY JOYCE

Katjia	Cat

DANIEL KAPAVIK

Baby Jane	Yorkshire Terrier

ALEX KARRAS

Joey	Shih Tzu
Lazlo	Dog

AL KASHA

Sweet Pea	Cat

GUNNAR KASSON

Balto	Malamute

HARRIS KATLEMAN

Mishka	King Charles Spaniel
Trillion	Labrador Retriever

STACI KEANAN

Fatty	Golden Retriever
Scarlet	Golden Retriever
Wally	Golden Retriever

GENERAL PHILIP KEARNY

Bayard	Horse
Decatur	Horse
Monmouth	Horse
Moscow	Horse

FRED KEATING

Snoopy	Boston Bulldog

BUSTER KEATON

Elmer	Saint Bernard

MICHAEL KEATON
Dusty   Border Collie
BRIAN KEITH
Colette   Dog
Paris   Dog
Wendel   Dog
HELEN KELLER
Kamikaze   Akita
Kenzan Go   Akita
SALLY KELLERMAN
Dylan   Llewellyn Setter
Roosevelt   Mixed Breed
DAVID KELLEY
Hogan   Dog
DR. HARVEY KELLOGG
Jadan   Horse
WILLIAM KELLOGG
Old Spot   Horse
GENE KELLY
Bambi   Sheltie
Ginger   Cockapoo
GRACE KELLY
Baba   Burro
Fanny Rhodesian Ridgeback
Oliver   Poodle
Timmy   Poodle
KAREN KELLY
Baby Dauphine   Toy Poodle
KATIE KELLY
Tom Cat   Cat
CAROLINE KENNEDY
Charlie   Welsh Terrier
Macaroni   Pony
Pushinka   Dog
Tex   Pony
Tom Kitten   Cat
White Tips   Dog

ETHEL KENNEDY
Pumpkin
          King Charles Spaniel
Souffle King Charles Spaniel
JOHN F. KENNEDY
Billy   Hamster
Blackie   Dog
Blackjack   Horse
Bluebell   Parakeet
Buddy   Dog
Butterfly   Dog
Clipper   German Shepherd
Debbie   Hamster
Maybelle   Parakeet
Moe   Doberman Pinscher
Robin   Canary
Streaker   Dog
Tom Terrific   Cat
Wolf   Irish Wolfhound
Zsa Zsa   Rabbit
JOHN F. KENNEDY, JR.
Leprechaun   Pony
Shannon
          Irish Cocker Spaniel
ROBERT F. KENNEDY
Croked Coconut Guinea Pig
Freckles   Dog
Shadrack   Salamander
DUKE OF KENT
Muff   Dog
CAPTAIN MYLES KEOGH
Comanche   Horse
Paddy   Horse
GEORGE & MARION KERBY
Neil   Saint Bernard
DEBORAH KERR
Guapa
          Pyrrenean Mountain Dog

Karty   Dog
Mas   Dog

CHARLES LAMB

Dash   Dog

MICHAEL LANDON

Bert   Dog
Buddy   Dog
Cobo   Dog
Laverne   Dog
Lucy   Dog
Mary   Dog
Mikie   Dog
Roxanne   Dog
Shirley   Dog
Wrinkles   Dog

WALTER SAVAGE LANDOR

Giallo   Pomeranian
Pomero   Pomeranian

ALLAN "ROCKY" LANE

Blackjack   Horse

ANDREW LANG

Ariel   Cat
Gyp   Cat
Master of Gray   Cat
Mr. Toby   Cat

PETER LAPIS

Hephastian   Keeshond

EARLE LARIMORE

Beebe   Siamese

JOHN LARROQUETTE

Bella   Boxer
Max   Rottweiler
Pluto   Golden Retriever

DAVID LASCHER

Chilly Willy   Cat

TOMMY LASORDA

Austin   Miniature Schnauzer

CYNDI LAUPER

Weasel   Cat

CAROL LAWRENCE

Boots   Cat
Chance   Shih Tzu
Charlie   Dog
Cleo   Yorkshire Terrier
Lance   German Shepherd
Miss Mouse
          Yorkshire Terrier
Odin   German Shepherd
Spot   German Shepherd

D. H. LAWRENCE

Aaron   Horse

GERTRUDE LAWRENCE

David   Siamese
Mackie   Dog
Wally   Siamese

JOEY LAWRENCE

Jack   Golden Retriever

STEVE LAWRENCE

Casey   Dog
Nugget   Dog
Roxy   Dog
Sonny   Dog

LEIGH LAWSON

Rascal   Cat

BARBARA LAZAROFF

Jaguar   Labrador Retriever
Melon   Irish Setter
Zandra   Dalmatian

CLORIS LEACHMAN

Bill   Dog
Captain Bobby   Dog
Joe   Dog

EDWARD LEAR

Flora   Dog
Foss   Cat

KING LEAR

Blanch	Dog
Sweetheart	Dog
Tray	Dog

MICHAEL LEARNED

Doris	Lhasa Apso

KELLY LEBROCK

Scratch	Cat

JEAN LECLERC

Kizmet	Cat

BRUCE LEE

Bobo	Great Dane
Riff	Schnauzer

CHRISTOPHER LEE

Tsar	Dog

DOROTHY LEE

Pappy	Dog

GENERAL FITZHUGH LEE

Nellie Gray	Horse

GENERAL "LIGHT HORSE" HARRY LEE

Magnolia	Stallion

GYPSY ROSE LEE

Bootsie	Poodle
Daisy	Guinea Pig
Jimmy	Guinea Pig
Molly	Rat
Mumshay	Spaniel
Samba	Guinea Pig
Sambo	Guinea Pig
Solly	Rat

ROBERT E. LEE

Ajax	Horse
Brown Roan	Horse
Creole	Horse
Grace Darling	Horse
Jim	Horse
Leonidas	Horse
Miss Long	Horse
Richmond	Horse
Santa Anna	Horse
Traveller	Horse

RUTA LEE

Kronen	Great Dane
Morris	Cat
Pinky	Cat
Sasha	Borzoi
Smoky	Angora

STAN LEE

Annabelle	British Bulldog
Pookie	Pug
Vera	Rottweiler

JOHN LEHMANN

Carlotta	Spaniel
Chico	Poodle

JANET LEIGH

George Brandt	Great Dane
Killer	Cat
Turkey	Cat

JENNIFER JASON LEIGH

Bessie	Cockapoo

VIVIEN LEIGH

Jason	Labrador Retriever
New	Cat
Nichols	Cat
Poo Jones	Siamese
Sebastian	Poodle

CHRIS LEMMON

Monroe	Cat

JACK LEMMON

Pepper	Pony

JOHN LENNON

Alice	Cat
Elvis	Cat
Merry	Akita

SEAN LENNON

Merry	Akita

JAY LENO

Cheeseler	Cat

DORIS LESSING

Black Cat	Cat
Mephistopheles	Cat

DAVID LETTERMAN

Bob	Dog
Stan	Dog

JERRY LEWIS

Angel	Shih Tzu
Lady	Shih Tzu

SHARI LEWIS

Lamb Chop	Lamb Puppet

ABRAHAM LINCOLN

Bob	Horse
Fido	Dog
Jack	Turkey
Jip	Dog
Nanko	Goat
Nanny	Goat
Old Bob	Horse
Pig	Pig
Robin	Horse

TAD LINCOLN

Tabby	Dog

MARK LINDSAY

Rusty	Dog
Scott	Doberman Pinscher
Zelda	Doberman Pinscher

PIA LINDSTROM

Kissa	Cat
Leonardo	Cat

ART LINKLETTER

Mai Tai	Cat

KING RICHARD THE LION-HEARTED

Alice-of-the-Night	Horse
Fauvel	Arabian
Lyard	Arabian

BEATRICE LITTLE

Lord Button	Pekingese

BOB LIVINGSTON

Starlight	Horse

HAROLD LLOYD

Bobby	Cocker Spaniel
Captain	Irish Setter

JUNE LOCKHART

Tony	Tibetan Spaniel

RICHARD LOCKRIDGE

Gin	Siamese
Martini	Siamese
Pete	Cat
Sherry	Siamese

PECHUEL LOESCHE

Muido	Cat

GENERAL JOHN LOGAN

Black Jack	Horse

JACK LONDON

Neuadd Hillside	Stallion
Possum	Mixed Breed
Rollo	Dog
Washoe Ban	Horse

LONE RANGER

Silver	Horse

GENERAL JAMES LONGSTREET

Hero	Horse

PIERRE LOTI

Moumoutte Blanche	Cat
Moumoutte Chinoise	Cat

GREG LOUGANIS

Bruno	Great Dane
Donna	Great Dane
Freeway	Great Dane
Lampchop	Great Dane

BARBARA MANDRELL
Boomer	Labrador Retriever
Peaches	Cat
Tasha	Yorkshire Terrier

BARRY MANILOW
Bagel	Beagle
Biscuit	Beagle

BARRY MANN
Geronimo	Cat
Oliver Junior	Cat
Quinn	Cat
Rocky	Cat
Saroya	Cat

JAYNE MANSFIELD
Powder Puff	Pekingese

KATHERINE MANSFIELD
Wingley	Cat

FREDRIC MARCH
Coco	Cocker Spaniel

MATTHEW MARGOLIS
Tillie	German Shepherd
Ulli	German Shepherd

CHEECH MARIN
Lillie	Dog

BERYL MARKHAM
Buller	Dog
Caesar	Bulldog

DAME ALICIA MARKOVA
Tinker	Cat

DUKE OF MARLBOROUGH
Jubilee Morn	Pekingese

GLADYS, DUCHESS OF MARLBOROUGH
Aloma	King Charles Spaniel
Babylas	King Charles Spaniel
Bacchus	King Charles Spaniel
Bettysan	King Charles Spaniel
Bneita	King Charles Spaniel
Daffodil	King Charles Spaniel
Dragee	King Charles Spaniel
Rita	King Charles Spaniel
Snowflake	King Charles Spaniel
Zona	King Charles Spaniel

GARRY MARSHALL
Cindy	Dog
Linus	Cocker Spaniel
Lucy	Cocker Spaniel

GENERAL GEORGE C. MARSHALL
Bones	Dog
Nato	Dog

PENNY MARSHALL
Betty	Dog
Handsome	Dog
Petey	Finch

DICK MARTIN
Bristol	Dog
Patty	Dog

JARED MARTIN
Loki	Dog

STEVE MARTIN
Dr. Carlton B. Forbes	Cat

PROFESSOR MARVEL
Sylvester	Horse

PRINCESS MARY
Patrick	Irish Wolfhound

JAMES MASON
Angus Silky	Siamese
Anna	Siamese
Baby	Cat

Cheo	Dog
Folly	Siamese
Gamma	Siamese
Lady Leeds	Cat
Sadie	Siamese
Skipper	Dog
Spider	Cat
Stink	Cat
Top Boy	Cat
Tree	Cat
Whitey	Tomcat
Zeke	Cat

PAMELA MASON

Angus Silky	Siamese
Anna	Siamese
Archibald Buchanan	Cat
Charlie	Siamese
Cloth Cap	Cat
Face	Cat
Miltie	Cat
Miss Hit	Cat
Mush	Cat
Petey	Cat
Princess Squaddle	Cat
Puff	Cat
Queen Di	Cat
Ruth	Cat
Tabitha Twichet	Tabby
Topboy	Cat
White Wicker	Cat
Whitey	Cat

RAYMOND MASSEY

Bunga	Alsatian

ROBBIN MASTERS

Apollo	Doberman Pinscher
Zeus	Doberman Pinscher

LOUIS B. MAYER

Alibhai	Horse

Beau Pere	Horse
Bull Reigh	Horse
Busher	Horse
Hemisphere	Horse
Honeymoon	Horse
Iron Maiden	Horse
Painted Beil	Horse

METRO GOLDWYN MAYER

Jackie	Lion
Leo	Lion

THE MAYFLOWER

Spannel	Dog

KEN MAYNARD

Sammy	Dog
Tarzan	Horse

KERMIT "TEX" MAYNARD

Rocky	Horse

ANNE MCCAFFREY

Mister Ed	Horse

LUCAS MCCAIN

Razor	Horse

PAUL MCCARTNEY

Martha	Old English Sheepdog

RUE MCCLANAHAN

Celestine	Cat
Panther	Cat

GENERAL GEORGE B. MCCLELLAN

Burns	Horse
Daniel Webster	Horse

PATRICIA MCCORMACK

Joey	Beagle
Sami	Beagle

TIM MCCOY

Ace	Horse
Baron	Horse
Midnight	Stallion
Pal	Horse

:::

Starlight   Horse

MARY MCDONOUGH
Nipper Dog   Dog
Samantha   Dog
Snoopy   Dog

RODDY MCDOWALL
Mr. Blue   Cat

MARY KATE MCGEEHAN
Bozo   Bird
Dixie   Dog
Scooter   Cairn Terrier

KELLY MCGILLIS
Cheyenne
    Australian Cattle Dog

SENATOR GEORGE MCGOVERN
Atticus   Dog

MAUREEN MCGOVERN
Calaban   German Shepherd
Magillacuddy
    German Shepherd
Nicky   Yorkshire Terrier

GARDNER MCKAY
Kenya   Cheetah
Pussycat   Sheepdog

PEGGY MCKAY
Cat Ballou   Cat
Cinema   Cat
Dingo   Dog
Ferdinand   Dog

WILLIAM MCKINLEY
Enrique DeLome   Cat
Valeriano Weyler   Cat
Washington Post   Parrot

ROD MCKUEN
Magic   Cat
Mr. Kelly   Sheepdog

EMILY MCLAUGHLIN
Tigger   Dog

KEN MCLAUGHLIN
Flicka   Horse
Thunderhead   Horse

ED MCMAHON
Hershey Bar   Cat
Monty   Cat
Queen Tut   Cat
W.C. Fields   Cat

PATRICK MCMANUS
Strange   Dog

JIMMY MCNICHOL
Heidi   Samoyed

KRISTY MCNICHOL
Lulu   Dog

PATRICIA MCPHERSON
Buckwheat   Cat
Flash   Cat
Sam   Springer Spaniel

STEVE MCQUEEN
Ringo   Horse

BRIAN MCRAE
Monster   Cat
O-Fer   Cat

GENERAL GEORGE MEADE
Baldy   Horse

JAYNE MEADOWS
Mr. T   Springer Spaniel

DENNIS THE MENACE
Ruff   Dog

BURGESS MEREDITH
Toby   Dog

LEE MERIWETHER
Black Beau   Cat
Daphne   Cat
Kitty Boo   Cat

KING MIDAS
Lampon   Dog

MONTE MONTANA
Rex — Horse
CLAYTON MOORE
Pandora — Persian
DEMI MOORE
Henry — Yorkshire Terrier
Junior — Australian Shepherd
Madison — Australian Shepherd
DUDLEY MOORE
Chelsea — Dog
Minka — Dog
Sadie — Cat
Schelsca — Dog
GENE MOORE
Daki — Cat
MARY TYLER MOORE
Dash — Golden Retriever
DisWilliam — Poodle
Dudley — Basset Griffon Vendeen
Maude — Poodle
Spike — Lobster
GENERAL JOHN HUNT MORGAN
Black Bess — Horse
Glencoe — Horse
LADY OTTOLINE MORRELL
Malbrouk — Cat
Socrates — Dog
JOE MORRISON
Boots — Dog
PAT MORROW
Billy — Horse
EARL OF MOUNTBATTEN
Kimberly — Labrador Retriever
MICKEY MOUSE
Pluto — Dog

SENATOR DANIEL P. MOYNIHAN
Whiskey — Terrier
MRS. CARLOYN MUIR
Scruffy — Dog
JEAN MUIR
Shandygaff — Scottish Terrier
JOHN MUIR
Stickeen — Mixed Breed
GREG MULLAVEY
Cleo — Cat
Crumpet — Cat
Hobo — Cat
Shinka — Great Dane
Tonka — Great Dane
Tooti — Great Dane
PAUL MUNI
Simon — Airedale Terrier
Toto — Dog
AUDIE MURPHY
Flying John — Horse
BILL MURRAY
Bark — Golden Retriever
JOHN MIDDLETON MURRAY
Athenaeum — Cat
Wingley — Cat
COUVE DE MURVILLE
Xenophon — Dachshund
BENITO MUSSOLINI
Fru-Fru — Arabian Stallion
JOE NAMATH
Poppet — Cat
ANNA LEE NATHAN
Hugo — Dog
MARTINA NAVRATILOVA
Killer Dog — Dog
Ruby — Dog
Yonex — Dog

ANNIE OAKLEY
Target   Horse
MERLE OBERON
Amber   Cat
Luke   Chow Chow
KING OLAF
Vigi   Dog
LAURENCE OLIVIER
New   Cat
ARISTOTLE ONASSIS
Djedda   Poodle
Pixie   Poodle
JACQUELINE ONASSIS
Danseuse   Horse
Sardar   Horse
YOKO ONO
Alice   Cat
Charo   Persian
Merry   Akita
Misha   Persian
Sascha   Persian
CHARLES OSGOOD
Fritz   Cat
DONNY OSMOND
Fuji   Akita
Lady   Dog
Lady II   German Shepherd
Lady III   Belgian Police Dog
Ossie   Dog
Pip   Labrador Retriever
JAY OSMOND
Chocolate Chip   Cat
Mugsy   Dog
MARIE OSMOND
Fuji   Akita
CATHERINE OXENBERG
Isolde   Cat
Tristan   Cat

JACK PAAR
Amani   Tiger
AL PACINO
Lucky   Dog
Suzie   Dog
THOMAS PAINE
Button   Horse
ARNOLD PALMER
Rieley   Golden Retriever
LILLI PALMER
William   Sealyham Terrier
SANCHO PANZA
Dapple   Horse
MICHAEL PARE
Cody   Golden Retriever
DOROTHY PARKER
Bunk   Dog
Daisy   Scottish Terrier
Eiko von Blutenberg
           Dachshund
Flic   Boxer
Misty   Dog
Nogi   Dog
Rags   Dog
Robinson   Dachshund
Timothy   Dandie Dinmont
Wolf   Bedlington Terrier
Woodrow Wilson
           Boston Terrier
JULIE PARRISH
Miss Pitty   Cat
Nastasha   Samoyed
DOLLY PARTON
Lickety Spitz   Finnish Spitz
Mark Spitz   Finnish Spitz
ELEANOR "CISSY" PATTERSON
Bo   Poodle
Butch   Poodle

❖

Todd Potter	Dog

SUZANNE PLESHETTE

Gypsy	Tibetan Terrier

EDGAR ALLAN POE

Catarina	Cat
Pluto	Cat

BRITT PONSET

Scar	Horse

ALEXANDER POPE

Bounce	Great Dane

COLE PORTER

Berthe	Dog
Pepe	Dog

MARKIE POST

Gypsy	Cat
Sybil	Cat

WILBUR POST

Mister Ed	Horse

BEATRIX POTTER

Chuleh	Pekingese
Fly	Sheepdog
Kep	Collie
Nip	Sheepdog
Sandy	Scottish Terrier
Spot	Spaniel
Tabitha Twitchit	Cat
Tom Kitten	Cat
Tzutsee	Pekingese

COLONEL SHERMAN POTTER

Sophie	Horse

PAULA POUNDSTONE

Haskell	Cat

DICK POWELL

Heathcliff	Cocker Spaniel

JANE POWELL

Ginger	Cat

WILLIAM POWELL

Fritzie	Dog

TYRONE POWER

Barakat	Horse
Lady	German Shepherd
Moonlight	Horse
Princess	Dog

STEFANIE POWERS

Bear	German Shepherd
Senor	Cat

AMY STOCK POYNTON

Zak	Cat

ELVIS PRESLEY

Bear	Horse
Brutus	Dog
Foxhugh	Maltese
Rising Sun	Palomino
Snoopy	Dog

LISA MARIE PRESLEY

Brutus	Dog
Snoopy	Dog

PRISCILLA PRESLEY

Domino	Horse
Honey	Dog

KELLY PRESTON

Max	Pig

SERGEANT WILLIAM PRESTON

Rex	Horse
Yukon King	Malamute

VINCENT PRICE

Albert the Good	Siamese
Brownie	Dog
Charles A. Greene	Parrot
Golden Blackie	Dog
Goldie	Dog
Hansie	Dachshund
Happy	Boston Bull Terrier
Joe	Dog
Johnny	English Bulldog
Josephine	Cat

MAUREEN REAGAN
Boxcar Willie   Mixed Breed
NANCY REAGAN
No Strings   Horse
Rex   King Charles Spaniel
RONALD REAGAN
Alamain   Arabian Stallion
Catalina   Horse
Freebo   Dog
Fuzzy   Belgian Sheepdog
Gualianko   Arabian
Lady   German Shepherd
Little Man   Horse
Lucky   Sheepdog
Millie   Labrador Retriever
Muffin   Cockapoo
Peggy   Irish Setter
Rex   King Charles Spaniel
Scotch   Scottish Terrier
Soda   Scottish Terrier
Taca   Siberian Husky
Victory   Golden Retriever
ROBERT REED
Mister Stubbs   Dog
DELLA REESE
All Spice   Dog
Cajun   Dog
Cinnamon   Dog
Nutmeg   Dog
Spice   Dog
Sugar   Dog
DAN REEVES
Hondo   Golden Retriever
Jake   Golden Retriever
STEVE REEVES
Red Cap 190   Bull
TIM REID
Rags   Dog

ED REINGOLD
Mimi   Cat
Willie   Cat
PAUL REISER
Frankie   Labrador Retriever
DUNCAN RENALDO
Diablo   Horse
AGNES REPPLIER
Agrippina   Cat
PAUL REVERE
Brown Beauty   Horse
BURT REYNOLDS
Astor   Dog
Bruiser   Dog
Clyde   Dog
Fred   Alligator
DEBBIE REYNOLDS
Killer   Poodle
CHRISTINA RICCI
Zert   Cat
KING RICHARD II
Mathe   Greyhound
Roan Barbary   Horse
KING RICHARD III
White Surrey   Horse
GOVERNOR ANN RICHARDS
Gracie   Parrot
SUSAN RICHARDSON
Honey Pie   Dog
Miss Chief   Cat
CARDINAL RICHELIEU
Felimare   Cat
Mimie Paillou   Cat
Perruque   Cat
Racan   Cat
Soumise   Cat
JASON JAMES RICHTER
Axl   Cat

WILL ROGERS

Bootlegger	Polo Pony
Chapel	Horse
Comanche	Horse
Cowboy	Horse
Cuba	Horse
Dodo	Horse
Dopey	Horse
Jocko	Sealyham Terrier
Monte Black	Horse
Robin	Horse
Soapsuds	Horse
Sundown	Polo Pony
Teddy	Horse

LITTLE ANNIE ROONEY

Zero	Mixed Breed

MICKEY ROONEY

General Felix	Cat

ALICE ROOSEVELT

Miss Emily Spinach	Snake
Sandy	Scottish Terrier

ELEANOR ROOSEVELT

Dot	Horse
Meggie	Dog

ETHEL ROOSEVELT

Fidelity	Horse

FRANKLIN DELANO ROOSEVELT

Blaze	Bull Mastiff
Budgy	Dog
Duffy	Scottish Terrier
Dutchess	Dog
Fala	Scottish Terrier
Major	German Shepherd
Marksman	Red Setter
Meggy	Scottish Terrier
New Deal	Horse
Peggy	Scottish Terrier
President	Great Dane

Tiny	Old English Sheepdog
Winks	Llewellyn Setter

TEDDY ROOSEVELT

Algonquin	Pony
Baron Spreckle	Hen
Bill	Horned Toad
Bishop Doan	Guinea Pig
Bleistein	Horse
Bob Evans	Guinea Pig
Dewey Junior	Guinea Pig
Dewey Senior	Guinea Pig
Dr. Johnson	Guinea Pig
Eli Yale	Macaw
Father O'Grady	Guinea Pig
Gem	Rat Terrier
General	Horse
Grey Dawn	Horse
Jack	Terrier
Jessie	Scottish Terrier
Jocko	Horse
Jonathan	Piebald Rat
Jonathan Edwards	Bear
Josiah	Badger
Judge	Horse
Manchu	Pekingese
Manitou	Horse
Maude	Pig
Pete	Bull Terrier
Peter	Rabbit
Quartz	Cat
Renown	Horse
Rollo	Saint Bernard
Root	Horse
Roswell	Horse
Rusty	Horse
Sailor Boy	Chesapeake Retriever
Skip	Mixed Breed
Slippers	Cat

RONNIE SCHELL
| Ethel | Airedale Terrier |
| Lucy | Airedale Terrier |

DINA SCHMIDT
| Beau | Great Dane |

MARGE SCHOTT
| Schottzie | Saint Bernard |

RICK SCHRODER
Grandview	Cat
Quentin	Cat
Smokey	Cat

REPRESENTATIVE PAT SCHROEDER
| Wolfie | Keeshond |

CHARLES SCHULTZ
| Andy | Dog |

ARNOLD SCHWARZENEGGER
| Conan | Labrador Retriever |
| Streudel | Labrador Retriever |

ALBERT SCHWEITZER
| Leonie | Antelope |
| Sizi | Cat |

BYRON SCOTT
| Fuji | Akita |
| Shira | Akita |

GENERAL WINFIELD SCOTT
Napoleon	Horse
Rolla	Horse
Washington	Horse

GEORGE C. SCOTT
| Max | Mastiff |

RANDOLPH SCOTT
| Bob | Collie |

SIR WALTER SCOTT
Camp	Dog
Hamlet	Greyhound
Hinse of Hinsefield	Tomcat
Maida	Mastiff

| Nimrod | Hound |
| Royal | Collie |

WILLARD SCOTT
| Ziggy | Cat |

MONICA SELES
| Astro | Yorkshire Terrier |

CONNIE SELLECCA
| Christy | Dalmatian |

TOM SELLECK
| Topper | Cocker Spaniel |

MAURICE SENDAK
Agamemnon	German Shepherd
Erda	German Shepherd
Io	Golden Retriever
Jennie	Sealyham Terrier
Runge	German Shepherd

US FOREST SERVICE
| Smokey | Bear |

DOC SEVERINSEN
| Travis | Cat |

LOUISE SHAFFER
Agnes	Poodle
Laverne	Sheepdog
Maxmillan	Shih Tzu

KID SHALEEN
| Smokey | Horse |

GENE SHALIT
| Junior | Cat |

WILLIAM SHATNER
Heidi	Doberman Pinscher
Kirk	Doberman Pinscher
Martika	Doberman Pinscher
Paris	Doberman Pinscher
Sterling	Doberman Pinscher
Sultan's Great Day	Stallion
Time Machine	Horse

☙ CELEBRITY INDEX

FRANK SINATRA

Leroy Brown	Labrador Retriever
Maf	Poodle
Miss Wiggles	Spaniel

MARC SINGER

Rufus	Golden Retriever

MARINA SIRTIS

Skilaki	Miniature Yorkie

CHIEF SITTING BULL

Blackie	Horse
Gray Ghost	Horse

RED SKELTON

Blondie	Cat
Freddie	Cat

CHRISTIAN SLATER

Barney	Dog

CHRISTOPHER SMART

Jeffrey	Cat

JACLYN SMITH

Albert	Poodle
Vivien Leigh	Poodle

KATE SMITH

Freckles	Dog
Sport	Cocker Spaniel

LIZ SMITH

Calypso	Dachshund
Luke	Abyssinian
Mister Ships	Cat
Odysseus	Dachshund
Suzanne	Burmese

OZZIE SMITH

Rusty	Cat

SHELLEY SMITH

Charlie	Siamese
Greta	Siamese
Max	Siamese

TARAN NOAH SMITH

Kiwi	Rat
Tino	Cat
Wiki	Rat

YEARDLEY SMITH

Betsy	Cat
Bonita	Cat
Clementine	Cat
Collette	Cat
Tubbs	Cat
Zapatos	Cat

CARRIE SNODGRESS

Bandit	Rottweiler

SNOOPY THE DOG

Woodstock	Bird

SUZANNE SOMERS

Bif	Goldfish
Chrissy	Cat
Muffy	Goldfish

ELKE SOMMER

Blackie	Dog
Hasi	Poodle

LOUISE SOREL

Gaby	Dog
Jiggs	Wheaton Terrier

ANN SOTHERN

Donnie	Scottish Terrier

DAVID SOUL

Dublin	Golden Retriever

ROBERT SOUTHEY

Bona Marietta	Cat
Hurlyburlybuss	Cat
Lord Nelson	Cat
Madame Bianchi	Cat
Madame Catalini	Cat
Othello	Cat
Ovid	Cat
Pulcheria	Cat
Rumpelstilzchen	Cat
Rumples	Cat

PATRICK STEWART

Bella	Cat
Sausage	Cat

ROY STEWART

Ranger	Horse

HARRIET BEECHER STOWE

Calvin	Maltese
Daisy	Dog
Tom, Jr.	Cat
Trip	Dog

SUSAN STRASBERG

Snow	Lhasa Apso
Sunshine	Collie

BARBRA STREISAND

Sadie	Toy Poodle
Sushie	Dog

SALLY STRUTHERS

Baba	Cat
Chester	Chow Chow
Chuckie	Chow Chow
Eddie	Chow Chow
Hailey	Newfoundland
Joan Pawford	Cat
Kitty Dearest	Cat
Scotty	Cat

GENERAL JEB STUART

Bullet	Horse
Chancellor	Horse
General	Horse
High Sky	Horse
Maryland	Horse
Skylark	Horse
Star of the East	Horse
Virginia	Horse

TOM SULLIVAN

Dinah	Dog

JACQUELINE SUSANN

Joseph	Poodle

Josephine	Miniature Poodle

GLORIA SWANSON

Poo	Pekingese

PATRICK SWAYZE

Br Ferouk Robert	Horse
Derek	Poodle

CHARLOTTE MAILLIARD SWIG

Stevie Wonderful	Cocker Spaniel

LORETTA SWIT

Croissant	Dog

CARL "ALFALFA" SWITZER

Corky	Dog

GLADYS TABER

Aladdin	Abyssinian
Amber	Abyssinian
Esme	Siamese
Tigger	Manx

WILLIAM HOWARD TAFT

Mooly Wooly	Cow
Pauline Wayne	Holstein Cow
Trevor	Irish Setter

CONSTANCE TALMADGE

Dinkey	Pomeranian

ARTHUR TAXIER

Beauty	Springer Spaniel
Roker	Springer Spaniel

ELIZABETH TAYLOR

Alvin	Parrot
Betty	Horse
Cleo	Siamese
Colonel Blimp	Terrier
Daisy	Yorkshire Terrier
E'en So	Pekingese
Elsa	Lhasa Apso
Gee Gee	Poodle
Jeepers Creepers	Cat

Jill	Cat
Mariposa	Shih Tsu
Nibbles	Chipmunk
Pee-Wee	Terrier
Reggie	Lhasa Apso
Sally	Yorkshire Terrier
Spot	Cocker Spaniel
Sugar	Dog
Thomas A. Becket	
	Yorkshire Terrier

ESTELLE TAYLOR

Charlie Chaplin	Cat

GENERAL MAXWELL D. TAYLOR

Rocky	Bear

JAMES TAYLOR

Florence	Cat
Ma-Zul	Cat
Mouse	Cat
Puffing	Cat
Tzing-Mao	Cat
Zula	Cat

LIZ TAYLOR

Charlie Brown	Burmese
Vincent	Cat

SHELLEY TAYLOR

Morgan	Cat
Ratzo	Cat

ZACHARY TAYLOR

Old Whitey	Horse

SHIRLEY TEMPLE

Ching Ching	Dog
Ching Ching II	Dog
Godzilla	Cat
Nicole	Cat
Poncho	Dog
Spunky	Horse

ALBERT PAYSON TERHUNE

Argus	Dog
Bobby	Dog
Break	Collie
Bruce	Dog
Chief	Collie
Explorer	Collie
Fair Ellen	Dog
Gray Dawn	Collie
Lad	Collie
Lady	Collie
Sunnybank	Dog
Sunnybank Jean	Dog
Sunnybank Sigurd	Dog
Thane	Collie
Wolf	Collie

ELLEN TERRY

Fussy	Dog

JOHN TESH

Christy	Dalmatian

TIFFANI-AMBER THIESSEN

Betty	
	Vietnamese Potbellied Pig
Bonnie	Golden Retriever
Clyde	Golden Retriever

GENERAL GEORGE THOMAS

Billy	Horse

ISIAH THOMAS

Cadillac	Cat

JONATHAN TAYLOR THOMAS

McCormick	Lhasa Apso
Samantha	Persian

RICHARD THOMAS

Charles	
	King Charles Spaniel
Henrietta	
	King Charles Spaniel

FRED THOMSON

Silver King	Horse

HENRY DAVID THOREAU

Min	Maltese

COURTNEY THORNE-SMITH

Ed	Dog
George	Dog

JAMES THURBER

Christabel	Poodle
Jeannie	Scottish Terrier
Jennie	Dog
Judge	Pug
Julie	Dog
Medve	Poodle
Muggs	Airedale Terrier
Rex	Bull Terrier
Samson	Water Spaniel
Sophie	Dog
Tessa	Dog

UMA THURMAN

Muffy	Chow Chow

CHERYL TIEGS

Martini	Wire Fox Terrier

GENE TIERNEY

Argus	Dog

ANN TODD

Whiskey	Dog

RICHARD TODD

Baron	Dog

THELMA TODD

White King	Dog

ALICE B. TOKLAS

Basket	Poodle

LILY TOMLIN

Tess	Norwich Terrier
Winston	Cat

MEL TORME

Spooky	Springer Spaniel

SPENCER TRACY

Slip Along	Polo Pony
Two Socks	Polo Pony

DANIEL J. TRAVANTI

Kitty	Cat
Oliver	Cat

MICHAEL J. TRAVANTI

Kitty	Cat

ARTHUR TREACHER

Belle	Yorkshire Terrier

SIR TRISTRAM

Passe Brewell	Horse

HECTOR OF TROY

Aethon	Horse

HARRY S. TRUMAN

Dewey's Goat	Goat
Feller	Dog
Mike	Irish Setter
Mike the Magicat	Cat
Tandy	Dog

IVANA TRUMP

Tiapka	Toy Poodle
Tiapka II	Poodle

AIME FELIX TSCHIFFELY

Gato	Horse
Mancho	Horse

TANYA TUCKER

Lucy	Bichon Frise

JANINE TURNER

Eclair	Poodle

KATHLEEN TURNER

McGee	Cat

LANA TURNER

Rowena	Horse

DICK TURPIN

Black Bess	Horse

MARK TWAIN

Appollinaris	Cat
Beelzebub	Cat
Blatherskite	Siamese

Buffalo Bill — Cat
Don't Know — Dog
I Know — Dog
Sour Mash — Cat
Tammany — Cat
You Know — Dog
Zoroaster — Cat

PRESIDENT JOHN TYLER

General — Horse
Johnny Ty — Canary

TOM TYLER

Ace — Horse
Baron — Horse

LIV ULLMANN

Pet — Dachshund

BLAIR UNDERWOOD

Kinga — German Shepherd
Shaka — German Shepherd

BRENDA VACCARO

Brentwood — Cocker Spaniel
Brindle — Belgian Sheepdog
Rosie — Cocker Spaniel
Skeets — Cocker Spaniel

ROGER VADIM

Clown — Dog

RUDOLPH VALENTINO

Haroun — Irish Wolfhound
Jadan — Horse
Kabar — Doberman Pinscher
Prince — German Shepherd

RUDY VALLEE

Mony — Dog

FRANKI VALLI

Allison — Cat
Bianca — Persian
Christopher — Persian

JOAN VAN ARK

Asole — Cat

Boulder — Old English Sheepdog
Carrream — Cat
El C. — Cat
Munson — Cat
Snug Harbor — Cat

EDDIE VAN HALEN

George — Burmese

CARL VAN VECHTEN

Feathers — Cat
Scheherazade — Cat

RIP VAN WINKLE

Wolf — Dog

ROBERT VAUGHN

Beans — Poodle
Pip — Poodle

REGINALD VELJOHNSON

Bear — Pug
Bebe — Pug
Brutus — Pug

EDDIE VELEZ

Blue Bandit — Siberian Husky
Dino — Siberian Husky
Red Bandit — Siberian Husky

GWEN VERDON

Fatrick — Cat
Feets Fossee — Cat
Tidbits — Cat

KATE VERNON

Mariko — Dog
Muffin — Cat
Prince Igor — Cat

QUEEN VICTORIA

Beppo — Pomeranian
Bully — Fawn Pug
Dash — King Charles Spaniel
Deckel — Dachshund
Fluffy — Pomeranian

Fyvie — Highland Pony
Gilda — Pomeranian
Islay — Dog
Laddie — Scottish Terrier
Lochnagar — Horse
Looty — Pekingese
Lulu — Pomeranian
Marco — Pomeranian
Monarch — Horse
Mop — Pomeranian
Nino — Pomeranian
Sharp — Labrador Retriever
Spot — Dog
Tartar — Horse
Turi — Poodle
Weldemann — Dachshund
White Heather — Cat

GORE VIDAL
Rat — Terrier

ABE VIGODA
Reggie — Dog

MIKE VITAR
Cindy — Parrot

JENNA VON OY
Sexy — Fish

JACK WAGNER
Elvis — Golden Retriever
Suzy — Golden Retriever

KATIE WAGNER
Casper — King Charles Spaniel
Oscar — West Highland Terrier

LINDSAY WAGNER
Cato — Cat

ROBERT WAGNER
Charlie — King Charles Spaniel

Chelsea — King Charles Spaniel
Dweezil — Cat
Fifi — Dog
Freeway — Dog
Loucouni — Horse
Mark — Cat
Moon — Cat
Pepe — Cat

JIMMY WAKELY
Sunset — Palomino

CHRISTOPHER WALKEN
Grace — Cat
Wolf — Abyssinian

BREE WALKER
Skeezix — Cat

NANCY WALKER
Lump — Abyssinian

RICK WALLACE
Hughie — Sheltie

HORACE WALPOLE
Selima — Cat
Zara — Cat

BARBARA WALTERS
Sale Gosse — Poodle
Zack — Dog

JANIS WARD
Choice — Cat

ANDY WARHOL
Amos — Dachshund
Archie — Dachshund
Katie — Cat

CHARLES DUDLEY WARNER
Calvin — Cat

MALCOLM-JAMAL WARNER
Makeba — Pit Bull
Mecca — Rottweiler

JAMES T. WEST
Cacao — Horse
Duke — Horse
JOHNNY WEST
Thunderbolt — Toy Horse
MAE WEST
Bad Boy — Monkey
NATHANAEL WEST
Julie — Hunting Dog
EDITH WHARTON
Miza — Pekingese
BARBARA WHINNERY
Miss Jenkins — Cat
BETTY WHITE
Bandit — Dog
Bandy — Dog
Binky — Pekingese
Bootie — Pekingese
Captain — Great Pyrenees
Chang — Pekingese
Cricket — Dog
Dancer — Poodle
Dinah — Golden Retriever
Emma — Poodle
Simba — Pekingese
Sooner — Dog
Stormy — Saint Bernard
Timmy's Kitty — Cat
Timothy — Cat
Toby — Poodle
Willie — Tabby
Woodstock — Parakeet
E. B. WHITE
Beppo — Irish Setter
Daisy — Scottish Terrier
Fred — Dachshund
Jones — Norwich Terrier
Mac — Dog

Mutt — Dog
T. H. WHITE
Brownie — Irish Setter
Killie — Irish Setter
Quince — Pointer
VANNA WHITE
Ashley — Cat
Rhett Butler — Cat
JOCK WHITNEY
Fred Astaire — Horse
JOHN GREENLEAF WHITTIER
Bathsheba — Cat
ELLA WHEELER WILCOX
Banjo — Chinchilla
ALONZO "MANLY" WILDER
Fly — Horse
BILLY WILDER
Chrystal — Dog
Inga — Dog
GENE WILDER
Sparkle — Dog
MICHAEL WILDING
Gee Gee — Poodle
MARY E. WILKINS
Augusta — Cat
ANSON WILLIAMS
Beau — Basset Hound
Country — Basset Hound
BILLY DEE WILLIAMS
Cho Cho — Cat
CINDY WILLIAMS
Chang — Cat
EDY WILLIAMS
Jimmmy — Dog
ESTHER WILLIAMS
Angie — Dog

HAL WILLIAMS

Miiko — Akita

ROBIN WILLIAMS

Big Sal — Parrot
Carl — Turtle
Duke — Dog

ROGER & LOUISE WILLIAMS

Lulu — Yorkshire Terrier

TENNESSEE WILLIAMS

Baby Doll — Bulldog
Buffo — Bulldog
Cornelius — Bulldog
Creature — Monkey
Gentleman Caller — Cat
Gigi — Boston Bulldog
Laurita — Parrot
Madame Sophia — Bulldog
Miss Brinda — Dog
Mr. Ava Gardner — Iguana
Mr. Moon — Bulldog
Satan — Belgian Sheepdog
Topaz — Cat

BRUCE WILLIS

Henry — Yorkshire Terrier
Junior — Australian Shepherd
Madison — Australian Shepherd

FLIP WILSON

Natasha — Australian Shepherd

JEANNIE WILSON

Precious — Cat

PRIME MINISTER HAROLD WILSON

Nemo — Siamese

WHIP WILSON

Silver Bullet — Horse

WOODROW WILSON

Caswell Laddie Boy — Airedale Terrier
Champion Tintern Tip Toe — Airedale Terrier
Davie — Airedale Terrier
Hamish — Old English Sheepdog
Laddie Buck — Airedale Terrier
Oh Boy — Bulldog
Old Ike — Ram
Puffins — Cat
Sandy — Airedale Terrier

MAJOR CHARLES EMERSON WINCHESTER III

Pegasus — Polo Pony

EDWARD, DUKE OF WINDSOR

Cora — Cairn Terrier
Davy Crockett — Pug
Disraeli — Pug
Gwen — Welsh Terrier
Jaggers — Cairn Terrier
Kate — Sealyham Terrier

OPRAH WINFREY

Arizona — Golden Retriever
Shane — Golden Retriever

DEBRA WINGER

Pete — German Shepherd

MIKE WINTERS

Lulu — Dog

P. G. WODEHOUSE

Webster — Cat

DAVID L. WOLPER

Moonbeam — Dog
Sunshine — Golden Retriever
Willie — Cat

BIONIC WOMAN

Max   Dog

NATALIE WOOD

Centime   Dog
Cricket   Sheepdog
Ginger   Cat
Jaws   Cat
Louis   Cat
Maggie   Cat
Oscar
         West Highland Terrier
Penny   Sheepdog
Potatoes   Dog

REV. J.G. WOOD

Pret   Cat

JOANNE WOODWARD

Griggs
       Louisianna Catahoulas
Harry   Wire Fox Terrier
Saki   Cat

VIRGINIA WOOLF

Othello   Spaniel
Pinker   Cocker Spaniel

WILLIAM WORDSWORTH

Dart   Greyhound
Music   Dog
Prince   Dog
Swallow   Dog

FAY WRAY

King Kong   Gorilla
Mr. Deeds   Dachshund

ROBIN WRIGHT

Bird   Shar-pei

VIVIAN WU

Fuller   American Eskimo

GRETCHEN WYLER

Daisy   Cat
Harold   Cat
Simba   Cat

JANE WYMAN

Scotch   Scottish Terrier
Soda   Scottish Terrier

VICTORIA WYNDHAM

Percy   Doberman Pinscher

TAMMY WYNETTE

Killer   Pomeranian

KEENAN WYNN

Pledge   Dog

POPE LEO XII

Micetto   Cat

KRISTI YAMAGUCHI

Skittles   Cat

MICHAEL YORK

Ming   Shih Tzu

SEAN YOUNG

Lacy   Terrier

JACK YOUNGBLOOD

Jet   Labrador Retriever

WILLIAM ZABKA

Buffy   Cocker Spaniel

PIA ZADORA

Mika   Dog
Shannon   Akita
Toki   Akita

DARRYL ZANUCK

Lisa   Yorkshire Terrier
Tina   Yorkshire Terrier

FRANCO ZEFFIRELLI

Bambina   Dog
Boboli
       Maremma Sheepdog

MAI ZETTERLING

Keeper   Irish Wolfhound
Lucius   Donkey

IAN ZIERING

Coty   Dog